LIVING MY FREAKIN' AMAZING LIFE

LIVING MY FREAKIN' AMAZING LIFE

Create the Life That's Perfect for YOU –
Anywhere in the World

Regina Huber

LIVING MY FREAKIN' AMAZING LIFE

Create the Life That's Perfect for YOU – Anywhere in the World

Published by Regina Huber

www.transformyourperformance.com

© 2024 Regina Huber

First Edition

ISBN 978-0-9889212-4-5 ebook

ISBN 978-0-9889212-6-9 paperback

Cover Design by Angie Alaya

I **dedicate** this book to anyone who showed up as a teacher and ally for my personal growth so far in this life and who still will: family, friends, schoolteachers, lovers, dance partners, coworkers, clients, business partners, civil servants and disservants, enemies, adversaries, traitors, and other passengers who crossed my path in this experience we call life. Without you, all the pages of this book would be empty, and my existence would be meaningless.

Table of Contents

Poem – Part 1

Someday, darling, we'll be gray

Darling, we'll be gray

And fret about the dreams we didn't chase

The roads not taken, the words unsaid,

The doors we closed, the paths we fled.

We'll wonder where those chances would've led,

And what we may have lost in fear and dread.

Foreword

I can't tell you how to live your best life.

No one can.

Because only you know.

What I *can* do is guide you to figure it out for yourself.

My goal with this book is two-fold: one, help you find the *freakin' amazingness* in your life as it is right now and two, inspire you to transform it into something truly extraordinary by acknowledging the magnificent (and limitless) potential in you that can make your life even more *freakin' amazing*.

Spoiler alert: Not everything in this book may seem *freakin' amazing* to you. Some of it may even completely *freak you out*.

See, my life isn't perfect.

It's perfect for *me*.

Why?

It's presented me the lessons I needed to grow and to enhance my consciousness – literally on a silver plate, without me asking for them… at least not that I was aware of. The truth is, even my most painful experiences provided me with an opportunity to not just grow and build resilience, but to *heal*. They held a mirror in front of me, inviting me to understand that everything in this mirror was a reflection of something that needed to be addressed and *healed*.

Not because something was wrong with me. But because we are all a piece of this overall Consciousness that we often describe as "Oneness" or "God," and my piece of this Consciousness must have somehow decided that this was the growth I wanted to contribute to the whole Consciousness… to "Oneness."

Every single person in my life that "inflicted pain or harm" on me, everyone who "created adversity" for me, has been my teacher and ally in growth, whether they were friends, family, schoolmates, lovers, business partners, or just "random people" I encountered on the subway or in the street. In reality, nothing is random, and there are no coincidences. Everything is just perfect synchronicity falling into place for us, even those unpleasant situations that we'd rather not have experienced – from the driver cutting into our lane to the piercing sting of betrayal.

My intention with this book is to ignite a spark in you that lights a fire of *freakin' amazingness* in every aspect of your life… so you get the most *freakin' amazing* value out of your time on Earth and can fully integrate this value into the piece of Consciousness that you are, heal the wounds of the past, feel awesome, and be continually mystified by life.

After much reflection on how to best serve you through my writing, I've decided to blend an entertaining personal biography with the valuable lessons for leadership of self and others that I've learned along the way. My aim is to offer insights that reassure you: there's nothing wrong with your life – or with you, and there never was. You have the power to create a *freakin' amazing life* for yourself, regardless of where you are or what your current circumstances might be. Through my experiences and takeaways, I hope to inspire you to embrace this potential and transform your own life in remarkable ways, which always starts with your perception of it.

You may find this process incredibly liberating, with your own sense of freedom expanding exponentially as you engage with it.

And you may find that you need a helping hand along the way. Then do feel free to reach out to me at regina@transformyourperformance.com and let's discuss the best options for you.

Every single page of this book has been written with you in mind.

Introduction
Leadership on Edge

Friends often say to me, "Regina, your life is packed with extraordinary adventures. You must write a book!" This idea planted a spark within me. I didn't just want to share stories; I wanted to share insights that resonate deeply with you, especially as a leader. This book is a reflection on how my adventures have shaped my approach to leadership and how these lessons can inspire you to live a life of bold decisions and resilient leadership.

I thrive in change. Venturing into the unknown, embracing uncertainty, and daring to take risks have been my greatest teachers. These experiences didn't just shape who I am; they taught me invaluable lessons in leading myself and others. Some risks paid off, while others led to profound growth and new opportunities. These stories are more than personal anecdotes; they are lessons in resilience, risk-taking, and leadership.

Growing up, adventure seemed to be in my blood. My dad, a nature enthusiast, had a passion for exploring – hiking, skiing, bungee jumping, even extremely strenuous ski tours... Being a farmer who also worked a full-time job, he didn't have much time on his hands to travel. However, he managed to set out on bike trips to Budapest and Rome on a simple 3-speed bike. His adventurous spirit inspired me, even though my escapades weren't always as athletic.

Despite my inner drive, I was the shyest kid in the village. As a little girl, my shyness was so intense that I would lock myself in my room with my brother to avoid going to kindergarten. The thought of interacting with other kids and being away from home was overwhelming. This created a constant inner conflict: my extreme shyness on the one hand, and my adventurous spirit on the other. I had big dreams but felt held back by my timidity, which often felt indistinguishable from being introverted. Later, personality tests revealed that I am an ambivert, so I have qualities of both the introvert and extrovert.

I was also a hopeless dreamer, always building grand castles in the air. I fantasized about living in a beautiful villa in Italy and traveling the world. But my shyness and lack of self-esteem made me question if it was even possible to conquer the world. Could someone like me, who struggled to find their voice, really achieve those dreams?

It turns out, my extreme shyness became my greatest strength. It gave me an air of mystery and depth. But most importantly, this shyness taught me courage. Courage isn't the absence of fear – it's doing it anyway... despite the fear! It's feeling the fear and moving forward anyway because moving forward feels right. It's taking risks, like traveling alone, and pushing boundaries even further by moving to a different country, a different continent. Each step, despite the fear, became a testament to my resilience and determination.

Over the years, I've found myself in some intense situations, like the time in Madrid when I encountered a knife-wielding stranger at an ATM or when I faced a gunman in Rio. These moments taught me about staying calm under pressure and thinking on my feet – serenity and composure being crucial skills for any leader.

But it's not just about the big, dramatic moments. Everyday adventures, whether in the streets of Johannesburg or the neighborhoods of Rio de Janeiro, have offered rich experiences and valuable lessons. It's these experiences that have made my life a treasure trove of stories and insights.

Resilience, a critical leadership trait, was often tested through moments of disappointment, betrayal, and loss. Whether it was the theft of sentimental items or the betrayal by a trusted business partner, these experiences taught me to turn sadness into strength and to forgive, especially myself. Resilience means stepping out of victim mode, dusting ourselves off after each stumble, and mustering the courage to start anew.

The beautiful moments, the whirlwind of living in diverse places from Munich to Madrid, São Paulo to Buenos Aires, Rio de Janeiro to New York, and Miami to Lyon, have filled my life with joy and excitement. My life on several continents and my extensive travels, including nine months in six African countries, allowed me to immerse myself in different languages and cultures, each teaching me new lessons in adaptability and culturally savvy leadership.

In March 2020, after returning from an extended stay in East Africa, I embraced a nomadic lifestyle, traveling across places like Playa del Carmen, Charleston, Jersey City, Weehawken, Munich, Paris, Miami Beach, Chicago, Phoenix, El Paso, Denver, Merritt Island, Tulum, Miami, and Zanzibar – and I may have forgotten a few – before deciding to split my time between Lyon, Miami, and New York City (for now, ha-ha). These experiences continue to unfold, promising new adventures and insights around every corner.

This book isn't just about my eclectic journey. It's about inspiring you to reflect on your own life and leadership. Life, with all its uncertainties, holds tremendous opportunities if you open your mind and heart to them.

Get a taste of the life you really want to live today! Not the life you think you *should* want. It's your birthright to experience freedom, fulfillment, and joy. What is it that you really, really want, deep down in your heart? Trust that you can achieve it because you can!

Lead yourself boldly and start living the life you've been dreaming of… now!

This won't make your life perfect, but it will make it perfect for *you*. It will be your very own unique, *Freakin' Amazing Life*.

Let the adventure begin.

Chapter 1
From the Bavarian Mountains to Leadership Peaks

Imagine a small farm in the heart of Bavaria, surrounded by just eight houses and with a beautiful view of the nearby Alps. This was my childhood world, a blend of rural charm, cow pies, and endless possibilities. My father, despite his roots as a farmer in this idyllic yet extremely demanding setting with long hours of work seven days a week, had a spark of adventure that took him on audacious tours on his simple bike and in the mountains. His spirit of adventure and love for the mountains left a profound impact on me, even as my mother often preferred the quiet life at home.

It wasn't just my father who had an adventurous streak — my siblings, and even my nephews, inherited it in their own unique ways. My brother Anton often takes long rides on his recumbent tricycle. Once, he hiked too far in the mountains and had to spend the night in the woods before heading down at dawn. My brother Franz is an avid mountain biker, while my sisters, Rosmarie and Martina, share a passion for both cycling and the mountains. My nephew Felix thrives on extreme sports, like downhill biking and bike races. His brother Tobias — an adventurer in his own right — once walked and skated all the way from Bavaria to Marseille in Southern France. Moritz, another nephew, has turned his love for music into a side gig that takes him to far-off places, like Cape Town. And through a documentary, I learned about Franz Heigermoser, a distant relative from my dad's side, who kayaked the entire Nile solo and climbed some of the world's highest peaks — just another fearless explorer in our family.

And so it is that Sunday hikes and winter skiing trips with my family were the highlights of my early years. My father, with his love for nature and sports, took us to the nearby mountains whenever he could. I would eagerly skip ahead on these hikes, always seeking the thrill of the unknown path. These early experiences taught me to lead myself, to be curious and unafraid of being a trailblazer.

Rainy Sundays found me in my room, an old atlas in hand, dreaming about far-off places like Italy, Brazil, Cameroon, and New York City. My parents, both born on farms, worked tirelessly to provide opportunities for their children that they themselves could only dream of. These dreams fueled my imagination and laid the groundwork for my future leadership journey.

After fourth grade, I started attending *Gymnasium* (high school) in a different town, where I met Trixi, who quickly became my best friend – a bond that has stood the test of time. In sports class, my insecurities were exacerbated by a scenario of being consistently picked last for team games. The process of selecting teams before a match was always a source of discomfort for me. The team captains, eager to win, prioritized the strongest players, usually leaving me and another classmate as their last option. My lack of speed in basketball and handball, coupled with subpar volleyball serves (in plain English, my serves sucked!), placed me in the league of the least attractive players. Picture this: as the team leaders called out names, mine was invariably the last one I heard. They picked everyone first but me! This was far from fun. Reminds me of the song "I'm still standing," but not in a good way.

As I grew older, adolescence brought its own set of challenges. Despite my shyness, I was always a bit of a rebel, and so I didn't always fit in. For example, the rules and tales of religion as well as some other traditions confused me. I didn't want to "play along" just because someone said so. I've always questioned what doesn't make sense to me (an attitude that's stayed with me all my life and has been particularly helpful – and healthy – in recent times). When I was a teenager, our religion (in my case, Roman Catholic) was stated in our IDs. While I respect everyone's religious views, I personally didn't identify with this religion at all, and I also didn't want to go to church on Sundays, as was customary for most people in our rural area at the time (although less in big cities). It just didn't feel right, and the message didn't resonate. As soon as I reached the legal age to request my official exclusion from the

Church, I did. If I remember well, that was around age 15 or 16. I even sacrificed my monthly allowance of then 40 deutschmarks to pay for the fee (it shouldn't have cost anything as I never asked to join in the first place!). Soon after, I received confirmation and a four-page survey inquiring about my reasons. I added eight sheets of paper and filled 12 (!) handwritten pages of solid reasons – from historical to current – why I didn't want to belong to this organization. After returning the questionnaire to the town hall, I never heard back from them. Back then, I hadn't really discovered a spiritual alternative for myself yet. In school, I opted for "Ethics" over "Religion" as soon as I could. I also explored other religions, but none of them really clicked for me. I felt a bit lost and confused. But over time, as I continued searching, I gradually developed a spiritual philosophy more aligned with what I know my essence and source to be.

In school, I had a strikingly handsome friend, Jo, who later became a model and likely had a crush on me. In school, we even shared the same piece of chewing gum, tossed it across the classroom between us (how gross, right?); we hung out at parties and playfully flirted, but that was about it. He was "too nice," which was one of my problems: I felt more attracted by the "bad boys" then. There was also Thomas, a neighbor a few years older than me, who had a profound influence on me. As a teenager, I was still struggling with my lack of confidence and lots of insecurities. That and my "bad boy" preference often led to relationships with boyfriends ending quickly. These experiences inspired me to reflect on the complexities of human relationships and the importance of understanding oneself – an essential lesson for any leader, though I wish I'd learned it in a more enjoyable way.

Despite the temptations and challenges of teenage life – drugs were quite common in the places we went dancing – my adventurous spirit and stubborn dreams kept me on a healthy path. I went on hitchhiking adventures, counted shooting stars while waiting on the side of the road, and even took a daring trip to Amsterdam at 16 with my friend Marion, spending most of the journey on trucks. These experiences taught me about risk management and resilience, crucial elements in my future leadership roles.

At 18, with my freshly obtained driver's license, I drove up all the way from the southeast of Germany through Alsace to the Bretagne in the north of France with my friend Lisi. In times without a GPS and with us having limited driving experience, mostly in the rural area we grew up in, we were proud to make it into Paris and out on the other side again after a short stop. Traveling on a budget, we sometimes slept in the car, tucked away behind some trees.

This was not the first time I´d sleep in the woods. We did this repeatedly on trips to Italy with another group of friends – Gabi, Karin, Marion, Peter and more – camping with only a sleeping bag and waking up faces bitten by mosquitoes and bodies bruised from the hard forest floor. We'd buy spaghetti and veggies and cook our meals on a small gas cooker. Those were our travels back in the day.

After *Gymnasium*, I moved to Munich to study Translation and Interpretation specializing in Economics. The transition from village to city life felt exciting but wasn't always easy. Loneliness crept in during weekends when my roommates went home to their families, but I was determined to embrace the city's vibrancy despite my limited finances as a student. Working part-time jobs and exploring Munich helped me shed my shyness and develop autonomy and problem-solving skills – key traits for any leader.

My first job after graduation was at the U.S. Embassy, but it felt too monotonous for my curious nature. I'm not the greatest fit for this type of workplace for sure. Seeking more, I joined a consulting firm, Boston Consulting Group (BCG), attracted by its global presence.

While working at BCG, I became good friends with Andrea, a colleague. We decided to book an amazing trip to Thailand together. We spent a few days in Bangkok, enjoying wild tuk-tuk rides, relaxing water taxis, and catching a show at the theater. Then we hopped on a small tourist bus and headed to Chiang Mai. It was that one time in my life I went for a package tour. We just had too little time to prepare, and traveling through the north of Thailand by ourselves would have been challenging. After returning to Bangkok, we decided to unwind for a few days at a beachside cottage on Koh Samui. Back then, Koh Samui was still a serene island with a newly built, small airport.

Another close friend I made at BCG was Regina. We didn't just share a name – we shared an office too, and we made a fantastic team. I truly enjoyed working in that environment, despite the intense pressure and demanding schedules. But the world was calling...

After two years, an opportunity in Spain came up. I quickly learned Spanish and moved to Madrid. This move taught me yet another crucial leadership lesson – embracing change and continuously learning. Each new language, city, and culture that would follow thereafter added value to my leadership toolkit.

Despite all the changes described in this book, one truth remained – I was a hopeless dreamer and always would be. Life, with all its twists and turns, never extinguished that flame. Deep inside, the little girl from Bavaria who once roamed the woods and dreamed beneath the stars persisted.

So much about my younger self. And my Freakin' Amazing Life had only just begun!

Each thrilling chapter that followed made me a stronger leader, both of myself and others. Today, "I'm still standing" has gained a completely new meaning for me.[1]

In the pages ahead, I'll share my stories and the lessons I've learned, hoping they inspire you to discover and embrace the wisdom you need to lead your own extraordinary life.

---

[1] Just to be clear: I'm not a fan of Elton John, even though I quote his song.

Chapter 2

Madrid Calling... and an Unexpected Twist

Lessons in Proactiveness, Adaptability, Setting Boundaries, and Imperfect Growth

It was the torching-hot summer air of Madrid that greeted me as I stepped off the plane, a sense of excitement coursing through my veins. At 26, I found myself at a crossroads, ready to embrace the unknown with open arms.

This first move abroad would forever alter the trajectory of my life… But how did I even get there? After all, I had studied English and French, a little "travel Italian" (and, oh well, Latin), but not Spanish. And I'd never felt particularly drawn to Spain. In fact, I had applied for jobs in New York City and Los Angeles (which I wasn't accepted for as I didn't have a green card). One day, my colleague Peter at Boston Consulting Group (BCG) told me about an opening in the Madrid office. I said: "But I don't even speak Spanish, Peter!" Peter just said: "You can learn that." – He was right!

I hopped on a plane to Madrid for an interview, feeling excited. The interview went well; only condition: "If you can speak Spanish within three months, the job is yours." Challenge accepted!

Determined to make it happen, I threw myself into learning Spanish like my life depended on it. I signed up for classes and spent every night studying, cramming in new vocabulary from Spanish newspapers. I was on a mission. And guess what? I spoke Spanish in record time! And this was how Madrid had me soon after.

Carmen, a colleague from the Madrid office, generously opened her doors for me to crash at her place while I hunted for an apartment. Soon enough, I landed a spot in the same neighborhood, Salamanca, setting me right in the heart of the city. Later, I hopped around a bit, trying out Canillejas, and Chamberí, with Chamberí quickly stealing my heart. It felt like home in a way no other place in Madrid did.

From my base in Madrid, I went on countless excursions to nearby villages and towns, initially relying on buses since I didn't have wheels of my own. There was this nifty travel agency on Gran Vía that organized Saturday day trips, and I was hooked from the get-go. Those excursions gave me a peek into Castilian life, architecture, and landscapes beyond the bustling streets of Madrid, and I soaked up every moment of it.

With each passing day, I immersed myself in the vibrant culture of Spain, honing my language skills and expanding my horizons in ways I never thought possible. Little did I know that this seemingly innocuous decision would lead to a leadership role within BCG – without any leadership background – no studies, no experience… and within only ten months after moving to Madrid and learning the language! It's maybe worth mentioning that there were two external candidates whose native language was Spanish and who did have relevant background, and I appreciate that someone must have recognized my potential – an attitude I soon applied in my own hiring practice as a leader and manager. The external recruiters overseeing the interviews also administered psychological tests, although I'm not familiar with the results. Nevertheless, I do know that I possess an "initiator" personality, which holds significant value in leadership roles.

This trait is incredibly valuable in a leadership context, as it indicates a proactive approach, the ability to inspire others, and the drive to spearhead new projects and ideas. An initiator isn't just someone who starts things; it's someone who envisions possibilities, takes decisive action, and encourages others to join in the journey.

In a leadership role, being an initiator means you're not waiting for opportunities to come to you; you're creating them. You're not just managing the status quo; you're constantly pushing boundaries, seeking improvements, and driving innovation. A proactive mindset allows for forward-thinking, which is key to staying ahead of any mediocrity.

The new role was a jump into the cold water, but the water soon warmed up, and I quickly grew into the seat behind my desk in my new office, adapting rapidly to my leadership responsibilities. Today, I see this experience as a testament to the transformative power of taking risks and seizing opportunities, paired with pure intentions.

What started as a plan to stay in Madrid for 12 months turned into a seven-year chapter! But my nomadic life had just begun… More about that later.

A few years into my Madrid life, BCG announced the opening of an office in Portugal. I was asked to have a pivotal role in this as the one coordinating the office build-out, as well as hiring, onboarding, and managing the entire business services team, in addition to the one in Madrid. This required me to learn Portuguese and to fly to Lisbon weekly to oversee the construction and interior design work and get all the ducks in a row for the opening – budgets, suppliers, operations, staff… An exciting outlook, as far as I was concerned – even though it added easily the hours of two or three additional workdays per week to my already very busy schedule.

And so it was that soon I found myself traveling regularly to Portugal, splitting my time between the two locations, hiring and training staff, managing teams, overseeing operations, and ensuring everything worked smoothly in the Madrid and Lisbon offices. At one time, I oversaw two office buildouts in both locations at the same time, as we also needed to add space for the Madrid office, while remodeling the existing space. It was an extremely intense time in my job, managing two interior design companies, contractors, budgets, and "work as usual," meaning, two offices and their teams. Later, I would use this new experience for the buildouts of my own brick-and-mortar businesses in Argentina and Brazil, although those were way more challenging… for different reasons. More about those later.

Madrid wasn't only about work, though! Nightlife is one of Madrid's special attractions, and it doesn't stop until dawn, with dinner often starting at 9pm and even later on weekends. If there is one city that never sleeps, it's Madrid! We'd often get stuck in traffic jams at 2am, and on weekends, it was challenging to hail a cab at 4 or 5am, with too many others competing for a ride home after a long night out.

Tapas are an invention I absolutely love! On hot summer evenings – and by hot, I mean 104 degrees Fahrenheit (40 degrees Celsius), often climbing to 118 Fahrenheit (48 Celsius) and occasionally higher during the day in summer, I wasn't usually in the mood for a large meal. While out for a few *cañas* (small beers) or some chilled white wine, we'd get a free *tapa* with each drink ordered. If we were still hungry, we'd share a *ración of boquerones en vinagre* (anchovies marinated in vinegar, olive oil, garlic, and parsley), *gambas al ajillo* (shrimp cooked in olive oil and garlic), *tortilla de patatas* (the typical potato omelet), or any other tempting choice on the rich Spanish *tapas* and *raciones* menu. *Tapas* are something I've definitely missed since leaving Spain!

On weekends, I'd just wander around, see where my feet took me. Sometimes I'd stumble upon these cute little squares I'd never noticed before. I'd follow my nose, stop for some tapas, maybe a beer or a glass of wine. Just living in the moment, you know? If Carmen was around, we'd meet up in the evening and keep the tapas train rolling. Sundays, I'd hit up one of the many indie movie theaters, watching flicks from all over in many different languages with subtitles – way more appealing than Hollywood movies, in my opinion. Madrid had so many cinemas, you couldn't run out of options, especially around Plaza de España. I've never found such a tremendous choice of great movies anywhere again!

Dance-wise, my time in Madrid was all about Salsa, Argentine Tango and Milonga, Merengue, Chacha, Sevillanas… the Spanish and Latino vibe. My work schedule was nuts, so I didn't get to dive deep into Flamenco like I wanted. But I managed to squeeze in some Sevillanas and Tango classes, and weekends were for Salsa in Malasaña, the neighborhood where nightlife never disappointed. And I got my first taste of Bachata in Madrid, hanging out with some Dominican folks.

It was also in Madrid that I made contact more regularly with contemporary African music, attending impressive performances like those by Cameroonian artist Manu Dibango. Dance aficionado that I am, I couldn't resist the allure of spectacular live shows, including mesmerizing performances by renowned international groups like Brazil's Grupo Corpo.

And, of course, no visit to Madrid was complete without indulging in the passionate rhythms of Flamenco – olé! I'll always cherish one particular memory of attending a Flamenco show with my dad and one of my sisters, Rosmarie, during their visit. My dad, with his love for the mountains, insisted on a trip to Segovia, and I eagerly seized the opportunity to showcase the enchanting charm of other nearby towns like Segovia, Toledo, and Salamanca. We created some cherished memories together, and I am forever grateful to have had the opportunity to give back to my dad, who had sacrificed so much of his wanderlust for me and my siblings.

Not much later, my time in Madrid was also marked by an incredibly sad event: My dad passed away suddenly in a car accident not far from home, back in Germany. It hit us hard, and it took me a while to fully grasp what had happened. My dad had always been the serene, steadfast anchor of our family, and somehow, I'd assumed he'd just stay with us forever or at least until he'd be very old. His passing sent a huge shockwave through my family, which can be felt to this day.

After some time had passed, my mom, who used to dread flying, flew out to visit, joined by one of her sisters with her husband. Together, we explored the olive-tree-dotted landscapes and towns surrounding Madrid. Seeing my mom finally experience a piece of my life abroad was lovely, and it was also bittersweet after losing my dad.

At work, apart from my friend Carmen, I had a solid crew – Gabriela, Helena, and Elsa. You could say, we were a formidable group of power women. Our evenings often stretched into the early hours, spent indulging in fine dining and lively conversation. We'd work hard, play hard, stay out late, and smoke like chimneys. Only to go back to work the next day as top professionals, after scant hours of sleep. Those were some evenings to remember indeed!

Thanks to my language and organizational skills, I found myself involved in coordinating BCG events in Barcelona and the Algarve, orchestrated from the corporate office in Boston. These engagements not only expanded my internal network, but also allowed me to explore the picturesque coastline of the Algarve alongside a colleague, immersing myself in the beauty of the region before the events commenced. It was a delightful opportunity to savor the unique charms of both Barcelona and the Algarve, enriching my understanding of these locations beyond my previous visits.

Amidst the vibrant rhythm of Madrid, some of my other siblings couldn't resist its pull. Both my youngest sister Martina, along with a friend, and one of my brothers, Franz, accompanied by his wife, made their way to the Spanish capital. Together, we soaked in the city's vibe, creating memorable moments amidst its lively culture. My sister and her friend fully embraced the Madrid nightlife, diving into after-hour parties that stretched into eleven hours of the following day. We all had a wonderful time together.

During my time in Spain, I ventured on extensive travels throughout the country, though I never quite made it to the Basque Country. Spain's diverse landscape and rich historical tapestry offered endless opportunities for exploration, from the arid plains surrounding Madrid, with its enchanting towns like Salamanca, Toledo, and Segovia, to the culture-rich cities of Barcelona, Pamplona, A Coruña, Santiago de Compostela, and down to the sun-kissed shores of Alicante, Valencia, and Málaga, to the southernmost point of Algeciras and extending all the way to Cáceres and to the border with Portugal, with Córdoba and Sevilla being some highlights as well, and many still missing in this list. While I'm writing this, I just realized how much I had traveled in Spain!

On some of these trips, I even tried my hand at horse-riding a few times, despite my lack of expertise and memories of childhood tumbles off a neighbor's horse still vivid in my mind (fortunately without any lasting harm).

My time with BCG afforded me excellent opportunities to dive even deeper into Spain's treasures. Luxurious trips, complete with stays in 5-star hotels and extensive golf courses (our boss was a golf aficionado), delectable cuisine, and thrilling excursions on sailing boats, opened up new vistas of the country for me. Through all these different experiences, I came to know Spain better than my own native Germany, having traversed most of its length and breadth.

I also had a not-so-pleasant "adventure" in Madrid: One night, I was out late with friends and found myself out of cash, needing money for a cab ride home. I walked to a brightly lit area with lots of car traffic (Madrid is a late-night city, always bustling, no matter the hour!), thinking it would be safer than a dark alley or side street. Just as I tried to withdraw money, a guy suddenly appeared next to me and held a knife to my chest, demanding the cash. I hadn't even withdrawn it yet, so in a reflex, I handed him my debit card and bolted. I ran toward the street, my heart pounding. Miraculously, I found just enough pesetas in the depth of my bag for a taxi home. Don't you love those bags with 1,000 inner pockets?

Despite the knife intermezzo and a more troubling personal ordeal involving being stalked by an ex-boyfriend, which contributed to my decision to leave, these were not the sole reasons. It was just time, according to my inner clock… seven years had passed. And despite these incidents, I chose to focus on the good memories and, as always, the lessons learned.

Leadership Wisdom – Key Takeaways

Anything Is Possible with Burning Desire

When you want something with enough burning desire, anything is possible. I learned Spanish and Portuguese quite quickly, but it wouldn't have happened this fast, had I not invested the necessary effort and time. Portuguese, in particular, is not an easy language to learn and understand, especially European Portuguese, which has intricate grammar and language etiquette.

The problem arises when you don't have that burning desire. A weak desire won't cut it – it must be strong and compelling. If your desire isn't intense enough, ask yourself if this is what you truly want, deep down in your heart, or if it's just something you think you "should want." It might be time for some soul-searching.

If you *do* have a burning desire but are *still* holding back, I urge you to take the leap – if not a leap, at least the first small step. Just do *something*! Now!

Adaptability Is Key

Living in Madrid marked my first venture into life abroad, a time when calling home was a luxury and flying back at whim was not an option. Despite being able to fly home once a year, it was not a feasible choice for spontaneous visits whenever I was in the mood for it.

The initial year was a whirlwind of cultural adjustment. While I had previously explored Italy and France, Spain unveiled a whole new world. Here, life unfolded predominantly in the streets, fueled by the extended periods of warmth throughout the year. The fashion sense was different, and conversations often revolved around the notion of "*de buena familia,*" signifying a background of privilege and status, a concept that had been somewhat foreign to me until then. In Germany, such distinctions were less pronounced in daily life.

This experience instilled in me the invaluable lesson of adaptability. It served as a training ground for future relocations to countries where social disparities were even more pronounced.

Of course, the reality has changed greatly in many countries since then, including Germany, and adaptability has become even more precious in our current times, especially adaptability paired with authenticity and courage on the other side of the coin; a combination indispensable for any sustainably effective leader.

Where might you need to adapt more? Conversely, where might you need to be more authentic to yourself? Striking this balance requires a considerable amount of self-reflection and self-assessment.

Proactiveness and Work Ethic Outperform Competition

For starters, in my world, there is no competition, period! We are all uniquely brilliant, and when we know, own, and show our brilliance, it more naturally propels us to where we want to be.

The only explanation I have for why I was chosen for my first management and leadership role is that I proactively made suggestions for improving local structures and processes. I was also extremely committed to always giving my best to ensure my project teams succeeded, and I showed flexibility when it came to working overtime. Given that the consultants occasionally used content from client presentations from the German offices, I even did translations over the weekend.

So, while I wasn't working toward a promotion and wasn't consciously competing against anyone, my dedication outshone the experience of external candidates, despite my lack of management or leadership background. Someone saw the potential in me... which, by the way, also helped me see the potential in people I'd hire later. In job candidates, I'd always look for attitude and potential over extensive experience.

When aiming for a role where you don't meet all the criteria, focus on powerfully positioning your unique strengths and potential. Mastering the art of positioning is crucial, and it's an area where I specialize as a coach, helping my clients excel.

Leading with Wabi-Sabi - The Power of Imperfect Growth

There is no perfect leadership. Leadership is never about perfection. When you lead from the heart with genuine intentions and maintain authenticity, you earn your team's respect more naturally. As you continue to lead, you'll develop any additional skills you need over time.

In leadership, embracing growth while acknowledging imperfections is essential. Wabi-Sabi teaches us that real strength comes from accepting flaws and valuing progress over unattainable perfection. Don't let the quest for perfection hold you or your team back. Celebrate every step forward and foster a culture where innovation thrives, without fear of making mistakes.

You are not expected to be perfect. Don't expect your team members to be perfect, either. Perfection in the sense of being 100% flawless is neither achievable nor expected from anyone. Just focus on doing your best and guiding your team towards growth and improvement. Being vulnerable and honest enough to admit your own mistakes will give your team permission to do the same, making necessary course corrections smoother.

Setting Boundaries Avoids Burnout

Over time, I began to realize that my employer was taking me and my hard work for granted. Fortunately, we didn't have cell phones back then, meaning I couldn't always be reached. However, my landline rang more than enough on Sunday mornings, making it really hard to disconnect and relax over the weekend. Just knowing that there could be yet another fire to put out over the weekend was stressful.

If I hadn't so badly wanted to add the Lisbon gig, I'd say I was being borderline exploited. However, I had signed myself up for that part, and I loved traveling to Lisbon, working in a different environment (I easily get bored and appreciate variety), and speaking Portuguese. Even if that meant getting up at 5am to catch my 7am flight once a week, coming back late that night, and working even longer overall schedules, the experience was worth it.

And after all, I was still learning to stand up for myself, so I must take at least part of the responsibility. Now, I know better, and you have the chance to learn from my experience: Don't let your manager or team take you for granted. Stand up for yourself when necessary. When you take on a new task, make sure to offload something else to avoid long-term overwhelm and burnout.

Are you being taken for granted in your professional environment? Here are some indicators: Is your workload overwhelming? Do you often find yourself picking up the slack? Are you constantly asked for favors? Are you always staying late or jumping in to solve issues while others relax, glad you're handling it... again?

Recognizing when you're taken for granted is crucial, and it often stems from our own behavior. Setting boundaries is a key self-leadership skill and sets a great example for your team when you do it as a leader.

*

In 1997, it was time for me to leave Madrid. As much as I loved this bustling city with its stunning architecture, vibrant nightlife, and charming little plazas – which I'd come to miss dearly – departure time had arrived. This departure was part of an intriguing pattern in my life, where significant changes seemed to come in chunks of seven or three-and-a-half years.

That very year, an unexpected opportunity landed on my desk: BCG was gearing up to establish an office in São Paulo. Given my proficiency in Portuguese, coupled with the fact that the partner spearheading this endeavor was a British colleague from my Madrid days, the stars seemed to align. Aware of my impending departure from Spain, he proposed that I lend a hand with the office setup and expansion for a couple of months. Brazil had always held a special allure for me, an irresistible pull that I couldn't ignore. Despite my initial plans to return to Germany, this was a once-in-a-lifetime opportunity that I simply couldn't pass up. And that's how in early summer 1997, my boarding pass didn't say Munich; it said São Paulo instead!

Chapter 3
Six-Month Stopover in São Paulo

Lessons in Seizing Opportunities and Embracing the Unknown

I arrived at São Paulo International Airport with a mix of excitement and nerves, scanning the crowds for my pickup service. No cell phone, no local coins to make a call – just my wits to figure things out. After exchanging some money to make a call, I spoke to the housekeeper. Speaking European Portuguese, which is quite different from Brazilian Portuguese, I managed to convey my need to get to the apartment. Eventually, I got the address, hailed a cab, and arrived.

The apartment was a sprawling penthouse with two floors, shared with my boss and two colleagues from Spain, along with their wives. We were in São Paulo to set up a new office, working out of a Regus office center while we were remodeling our own space. I was in charge of coordinating the buildout, training staff, and hiring together with the local office manager. Just like in Madrid, our days were long, often stretching late into the evening.

It soon dawned on me that my intended stay would extend well past the initially planned two months, ultimately spanning nearly six months in total. Without a car and only packing for what was supposed to be a couple of months, I needed to stock up on clothes. Sometimes, I would take a bus to a distant shopping mall. São Paulo, a megacity with around 20 million inhabitants, had a complex bus system, but somehow, I managed. One night, coming back around 10 pm from shopping, I took the wrong bus and ended up heading towards downtown – not the safest place at night. I asked the bus driver for help, and he suggested I get off at the next stop to catch a different bus to my neighborhood, Itaim Bibi. This meant walking through an underpass to the other side of a multi-lane street – definitely not the best idea late at night in São Paulo. But it seemed like I had no better choice, so I ventured into the long, dimly lit tunnel with its grimy walls, hoping to make it through to the other side alive and unscathed. The tunnel seemed to stretch on forever, its darkness amplified by the absence of any light at the far end... Literally, there was no light at the end of the tunnel; that street certainly wasn't lit up like Times Square! I was trying to keep my mind off all the bad things that could possibly happen in there... To stave off the fear, I imagined a protective bubble around me – a mental trick I'd often use when I was out late at night in the streets of high-crime cities like São Paulo. Trusting in this imaginary shield, I pressed on.

Thankfully, I made it safely to the other bus and got home. In a city where cars are allowed to run red lights at night for safety and police cars are stationed at intersections on Avenida Nove de Julho during the night to keep drivers safe, you learn to be vigilant, especially as a pedestrian.

In the early days, my colleagues would tease me, albeit playfully, about my European Portuguese accent. The lady I collaborated with closely, Lucia, who soon became a dear friend, would jestingly introduce me as "Regina – ela fala português de Portugal," mimicking a heavy Portuguese accent. This lighthearted banter inspired me to swiftly adapt my accent and vocabulary to better align with the local speech patterns, a decision that would later prove advantageous (although I still feel a special affection for European Portuguese as well). When I eventually relocated to Brazil, this time to Rio, I found my adjusted pronunciation and vocabulary to be beneficial once again, despite the subtle differences in pronunciation between *cariocas* (residents of Rio) and *paulistas* (residents of São Paulo).

São Paulo is famous for its high-end restaurants from around the world, including Japanese eateries in the Liberdade neighborhood and fantastic local spots in Vila Madalena. Vila Madalena is one of the trendiest areas, filled with funky shops, fashionable bars, and avant-garde art galleries. The BCG team offered frequent opportunities to savor lots of these city gems, including generous invitations to the best restaurants in town, especially as my boss was committed to exploring

24

new restaurants every single week, and my colleague Lucia was an expert in the restaurant scene with the different cuisines.

Naturally, dance was also on my mind while in São Paulo. Eager to immerse myself, I did some research and enrolled in a few *Samba de Pagode* partner dance classes. This was a very particular style of dancing samba, specifically in a partner format, which I later never found again in Rio de Janeiro or anywhere else.

One of our memorable trips from São Paulo was to the mountains of Teresópolis in Rio de Janeiro state for rappelling and river rafting. We traveled overnight by bus and started our adventure with a hike to a massive rock for our first rappelling experience. It was slightly intimidating but manageable. From there, we hiked to a 35-meter waterfall. While many stopped there, we continued to the top, crossing some daunting, inclined rock slabs. As I peered over the edge of the rock where the rappelling descent began, I felt a surge of fear. The thought of stepping into what felt like "void" was truly frightening. What if the rope broke? What if it wasn't properly secured? Watching even the most confident go silent and ashen-faced before their descent, I decided to retreat. Sneakily, so no one would notice, I started back on the path, only to find that crossing the inclined rock area was much scarier in the opposite direction. Strangely, leaning against the inclination on my right side felt safer than on my left, even with the abyss on my right. I was almost relieved when one of the guides came to my rescue – but not to help me return. Instead, he convinced me to try rappelling down the waterfall. I agreed, but being the last one to descend didn't make it easier. Watching everyone before me go pale didn't help!

Even just looking at that overhang was terrifying! Eventually, it was my turn. Truth be told, the initial steps were nerve-wracking: Moving into a horizontal position, my feet finding their place on the side of the rock… My life literally was hanging on a string!

But once I settled into the rhythm, it was exhilarating, and after a few more steps, I was feeling more at ease handling my ropes. I descended with stunning views of the waterfall, making my way down on my seat of ropes, feeling a sense of pride for conquering my fear.

After a long hike back to our lodge, partly in the dark, we enjoyed a well-deserved dinner. The next day, we went river rafting. Our team, eager for adventure, repeatedly paddled against the stream, which eventually tipped our boat over. I found myself under the boat, seeing only bubbly water around me and the boat above me. It was not easy to get out quickly, surrounded by the boat's hull on all sides. It was a scary moment, but the guide pulled me out, and we righted the boat. A bit exhausted from the momentary shock, yet glad that I was back in the boat rather than under it, I felt hungry!

For lunch, we used the overturned boat as a table, feasting on tropical fruits and snacks before paddling to our final destination. The next day, my arms were stiff from the exertion, but the experience was all worth it.

Returning to the megacity also meant back to long hours at the office, ensuring our imminent move to our new space in Vila Olímpia went smoothly. This included hiring the ideal candidates to fill the immediate job vacancies, onboarding and training them. My colleague Lucia and I didn't just make an excellent team for this; we also became friends along the way. Through her, I experienced different facets of the city, such as an upscale country club.

Just like in Madrid, where I'd been working with interior designers to add a floor and remodel the existing space on the 5th floor, and in Lisbon, where I oversaw the buildout of the first office located on Av. da Liberdade, it was thrilling to witness the office space evolve from a raw, empty shell to a beautifully furnished and equipped workspace, ready for our team to move into.

From São Paulo, we joined the BCG Buenos Aires office on a company outing to Patagonia, where we explored glaciers with spikes on our shoes and took a cold but exhilarating boat trip on a glacier lake. We also enjoyed some exceptional scenery, which included large flocks of sheep grazing in the fields. We even visited a farm where we watched sheep being sheared and saw how their woolen fleece was prepared for processing. The legendary BCG office outings in South America were just as lively as those in Spain, with plenty of intense partying included.

Towards the end of my stay, I took a week off to visit Natal in Rio Grande do Norte. Exploring the dunes and surrounding areas was an unforgettable experience. Afterward, I returned to São Paulo before heading to Buenos Aires for a few weeks to assist the local office manager. Though I was asked to extend my stay, I felt it was time to return to Germany, visit my family, and start the next chapter in Munich after over seven years abroad.

Leadership Wisdom – Key Takeaways

Seizing Opportunities, Embracing the Unknown, and Taking Risks Lead to Pivotal Moments

If I hadn't seized the opportunity to spend time in São Paulo, the trajectory of my life might have taken a completely different course. Sure, returning home would have provided comfort and familiarity, but the allure of a new challenge was simply too irresistible to ignore. São Paulo seemed enticing as one of the world's largest cities, a bustling metropolis teeming with opportunities and adventures waiting to be embraced. It wasn't just about navigating a new "battleground"; it was an opportunity for personal and professional growth. Immersing myself in this vibrant city meant honing my language skills, navigating cultural nuances, and acquiring new competencies that would prove invaluable in my future endeavors. Each day presented a chance to expand my horizons, to learn from the diverse patchwork of experiences that São Paulo had to offer.

Stepping into that overhang in Teresópolis was a whole other dimension. Because while I have always felt adventurous enough to explore new locations, I was never much into high-risk sports, unlike my dad or some of my siblings and nephews.

In hindsight, it's clear that these decisions to embrace the unknown were pivotal, shaping not just my career path and my determination as a leader, but also fostering personal resilience and adaptability that would serve me well in years to come.

This stay didn't just broaden my external horizons; it also expanded my internal ones. It sparked new dimensions of thought, opening my mind in ways I hadn't imagined before.

Life itself is an adventure. Are you ready to live it?

- What opportunity is calling out to you right now, waiting for you to seize it – big or small? Don't put it off or you might miss it. The time is now! Take the first step, or it may be too late. The best opportunities often vanish very quickly.
- What risk must you embrace to elevate your career, your business, your vision to the next level? Picture the boundless possibilities that the unknown holds for you! Your life is too precious to let them slip by unexplored.
- Say goodbye to fear and hello to courage! Every decision you make is a steppingstone toward your future self. The unknown is not something to fear, but a fertile ground where your dreams can take root and flourish. By stepping out of your convenience zone (it's not really a "comfort zone," is it? Because I bet it's not that comfortable to be in a limiting place) and embracing uncertainty, you open the door to new experiences, growth, and transformation.

Think about it: what if the opportunity you're hesitating to take is the very catalyst for your breakthrough? What if the risk you're contemplating is the bridge to your greatest achievements? Often, the most significant growth happens when we dare to venture into uncharted territories. This is where you transcend your limitations, where your potential unfolds.

Imagine the exhilaration of stepping into a new role, launching that innovative project, or taking a bold step in your business. Envision the ripple effects of your courage, not just on your life but on those around you – when they see you lead in this way. Your bravery can inspire others to follow suit, creating a wave of positive change. It's what leaders do! Go for it!

*

Flying back to Munich stirred a mix of emotions: anticipation to reunite with family and friends, looking forward to shopping at the Viktualienmarkt (the famous open-air food market), cozying up in cafés, and savoring meals at favorite restaurants. Munich's charm with its scenic cityscapes, majestic nearby mountains, and serene lakes is certainly worth some praise. Yet, I was keenly aware that returning wouldn't recreate the initial thrill of living there for the first time. Also, I already missed Madrid's vibrant energy and the warmer climate. I've never been a fan of the cold. Departing from a city like Madrid where I had spent seven years was not without its emotional weight.

Chapter 4

Back in the World City with a Heart

Lessons in Self-Discovery and the Importance of Negotiation

In December 1997, I took a plane home to Germany. My first station was the house I grew up in, visiting family, and from there, I moved into a beautiful apartment in the Haidhausen neighborhood of Munich, not far from where I'd left over seven years earlier. It was an interesting time of readjusting in the "City of Art and Beer." While I appreciated many aspects of my original home country, I missed the *ambiente* of Madrid and Lisbon greatly. Munich seemed so small now, and it was January and cold, which didn't help.

However, it wasn't long before I was enjoying evenings out dancing, reconnecting with old friends, and making new ones. I was offered a role coordinating BCG's global intranet buildout as well as an intricate digital system for everything related to Europe-based staff, from recruiting to training to staffing to career development. What I liked the most about the job was the travel – it took me to BCG offices all over Europe to train users. Plus, I got to work mostly in English, but also some Spanish and Portuguese when visiting the Iberian offices, which was a nice perk.

As I was involved in both the content and IT aspects of the project, I reported to two bosses: one based in the corporate office in Boston and another in Munich. On one occasion, my Boston boss invited me to join a trip to the Bahamas for a project meeting. However, my Munich boss decided there wasn't enough budget for me to go, opting to take others from his team instead, with whom he had a closer relationship.

This wasn't the only instance where I clashed with him; his macho and condescending personality didn't sit well with me. I found it challenging to connect with him and his boss, and their office politics didn't make things easier. What exacerbated the situation was their mishandling of my compensation package, from which they removed my pension fund, which, I must emphasize, did not align with typical BCG policy. I must admit that at the time, I wasn't the best when it came to negotiating for myself. For others, absolutely! For myself, not so much.

On the positive side, the travel throughout Europe was still required and uncontested... But I didn't only travel for work...

During my first year back home, I took a trip to Cuba with my youngest sister Martina. Despite it being hurricane season, we were undeterred. Havana welcomed us warmly, and our adventure took us across the island on a bus tour covering Pinar del Río, Matanzas, Santa Clara, Cienfuegos, and Trinidad, among other places.

There was an amusing twist during our tour when the bus driver seemed more interested in me than the road ahead, constantly checking the rearview mirror! He must have had a crush on me! We ended up becoming good friends and shared a memorable night over glasses of delicious Cuban rum outside our cabin. After exploring a large portion of the island, we hunkered down in Varadero as the hurricane approached. Despite the storm's anticipation, we managed to salsa dance with newfound local friends and enjoyed a lobster dinner at a local family's home.

When the hurricane eventually hit, we followed hotel instructions like taping windows and spent a memorable night playing cards by candlelight – the Cuban way, with rum and cigars. The next day, the streets were flooded, and activities were limited, but we made the most of our remaining time in Cuba before heading back home, feeling exhilarated by an unforgettable trip.

Later, I traveled to Brazil with my friend Mary Ann. We started with a few days in São Paulo and then moved on to Rio de Janeiro. One morning, as we were having breakfast at our Copacabana hotel on Av. Princesa Isabel, we heard gunshots outside. Remarkably, this was my second visit to Rio and the second time I had witnessed a shooting, which however didn't deter me from moving there years later.

From Rio, we journeyed to Salvador da Bahia, where we celebrated New Year's Eve with breathtaking fireworks and participated in the Brazilian tradition of placing white flowers on the beach and in the ocean. We also explored pristine beaches near Salvador, such as Praia do Forte and Arembepe. The cuisine in the Northeast of Brazil has always been my favorite, featuring delectable dishes like *moqueca* (seafood stew), *bobó de camarão* (shrimp/cassava stew), the best *peixe grelhado com pimenta* (grilled fish with tiny chili peppers in oil) I've ever had, especially when freshly barbecued on the beach or on Itaparica Island, and *acarajé*, a distinctive and flavorful treat, often freshly prepared by traditionally dressed women in the vibrant streets of Salvador.

From Bahia, we flew to Manaus in the Amazon region. The next day, we traveled on to a lodge in the wilderness, from where we went on long canoe rides, spotting the legendary pink river dolphins, watching baby crocodiles at night, and catching small barracuda-like fish with sharp teeth, which we then enjoyed for dinner. The mischievous monkeys there would steal anything they could get their hands on – from our cups, which they'd drink from before tossing them over their own shoulders *nazdorovie*-style, to any unattended food or bags. After reveling in the abundant natural beauty, we lingered a few more days in Manaus before heading back to the coast and eventually returning to Munich.

My friend Marietta and I once flew to Buenos Aires, then took a bus to Cordoba before traveling on to the Catamarca, Salta, and Jujuy Provinces in northwestern Argentina – an area I find incredibly fascinating. We explored Catamarca, Cafayate, San Salvador de Jujuy, Tilcara, and Salta. The landscapes were breathtaking, especially the colorful mountains, el Cierro de los Siete Colores, in Tilcara, but also our walk through vast expanses of towering cacti, which we reached by riding in the open part of a truck one day.

While living in Munich, dance-wise, I immersed myself in Salsa, Argentine Tango, and Samba no Pé, squeezing it into my schedule whenever possible. For Samba, I took weekly classes with Martinho, a Brazilian professional dancer from Salvador. My favorite Tango partner was a Turkish guy back then, and Salsa nights out with José from Galapagos sometimes meant catching just an hour of sleep before taking a cold shower and heading to the office.

But soon, the work became monotonous. As mentioned above, there were some unpleasant office politics on the tech side of the team, and I felt cheated out of my pension fund contributions when signing my work agreement. Negotiating wasn't my strong suit back then, but it should have been handled differently. Overall, I didn't feel as respected as I had in my previous job. My passion for the projects waned, and I found myself wondering what was next.

Then, an email from Argentina hit my inbox: An Argentine BCG alum I knew from the Madrid office had founded a start-up: Deremate, which was similar to eBay, but for Latin America and Florida. He suggested I join his team as the Training & Internal Communication Coordinator. They were looking for someone who spoke both Spanish and Portuguese. I was all ears.

Just about nine months earlier, I had moved to a lovely apartment in fashionable yet cozy Glockenbachviertel, a part of the Munich Isarvorstadt neighborhood, which I loved. But the pull was too strong. I just had to follow this nudge from the Universe.

Long story short, I followed my heart, packed up, quit my job at BCG, and flew all the way to Buenos Aires once again. I didn't give up my apartment, though, as my accommodation in Buenos Aires was covered by the company, and my best friend wanted to rent my Munich place part-time for her dance outings in Munich. Also, this was a contract, and not an employment offer. So, in August 2000, one of my sisters and two friends took me to the airport, where I had a last wheat beer before boarding the plane and leaving the capital of beers.

Leadership Wisdom – Key Takeaways

From the Discovery of New Places to the Discovery of Self

My takeaway from this chapter crystallized around the realization that I am inherently drawn to exploring new places and immersing myself in diverse cultures. I'm literally "made for it." While I cherish my roots and maintain a deep connection with my family despite the geographical distance, and I profoundly appreciate the beauty of the area I grew up in, there's an undeniable calling within me to traverse new horizons. It's a journey of self-discovery – a fusion of internal and external exploration – that has nurtured my self-awareness, which is a fundamental precursor to effective self-leadership. Indeed, all leadership begins with oneself; self-awareness precedes the ability to lead others.

For me, self-awareness has evolved through a mosaic of eclectic experiences, each contributing to my growth and development as a leader of myself. Engaging with different people, places, and cultures has not only broadened my understanding of the world but has also provided profound insights into my own identity, and it's helped my self-actualization process. It's been a voyage of self-exploration intertwined with a deeper comprehension of the human experience and the essence of what it means to be human.

Reflect on this: How well do you know yourself? Explore further and see where your own journey of self-awareness can take you. Grab a notepad and pen and journal about your experiences, how they've shaped your self-awareness. Then think about how these insights can benefit your future.

Negotiating Pays Off

That was just the beginning of a series of eye-opening experiences I had due to not negotiating my compensation effectively. Later, I made the same mistake, compounded by insufficient research, and this ended up costing me significantly over the years.

However, these setbacks spurred me to develop the Negotiate Your Dream Salary™ framework and launch my Dream Salary online course in my coaching business. Through these resources, I've helped numerous clients to negotiate salaries far beyond their expectations.

Are you making some of the same mistakes I made when accepting a new job or salary offer?

- Giving in too quickly to concessions: Agreeing to changes or reductions requested by the employer without sufficient negotiation
- Trading away compensation elements: Compromising on specific parts of your compensation package too readily instead of requesting the full range of benefits you deserve
- Accepting lower pay: Settling for a salary that is below your expectations or market value
- Underestimating the value of your work: Not fully recognizing and asserting your value in the job market
- Letting your lack of perceived self-worth interfere with your negotiation power
- Not negotiating at all: Accepting the initial offer without attempting to negotiate for better terms.

My advice today: Negotiate the heck out of your compensation! Don't settle until you're genuinely satisfied. This approach not only prevents future frustration but also guards against self-resentment. Remember, even benefits like a pension fund, which may only materialize in the future, are crucial. It's always better to have them than to go without. My Dream Salary online course can help you get the salary you want and deserve as you shift your mindset, learn to position yourself and effectively address objections.

*

Saying goodbye to my sister Martina and my friends Marietta, Mary Ann, and Adriane at Munich's Franz Josef Strauß Airport, as I walked into the security area, I couldn't help but think, "I knew it! I always knew I would leave again. Who was I kidding? It was inevitable!" I'd always felt like I had one foot outside of Germany, and now, the moment had arrived to place both my legs on the South American continent again. However, it is also true that I hadn't suspected this to happen so quickly. Opportunities arise when you least expect them…

Chapter 5
Starting Up in Buenos Aires &
Backpacking in Central America

Lessons in Resourcefulness

In Buenos Aires, I shared a spacious flat in a central neighborhood with my Mexican colleague

Pato, and we became good friends… still are. We later reconnected in New York, and I also visited her in Mexico City after spending time with Shamans in Apaseo el Alto, about 140 miles northwest of the capital, as well as in San Miguel de Allende and Santiago del Querétaro. I had a lovely time at her home, exploring parts of the city I had never seen before as well as revisiting the houses of Frida Kahlo and Diego Rivera, the famous Mexican painters. But I digress...

In the capital of Tango, I took Argentine Tango classes with Ernesto and Norma, where I also met my dear friends Mónica and Gianna, explored various milongas, and found another dear friend-to-be from Brazil, dance instructor Claudio. He introduced me to Brazilian Zouk-lambada dancing and later traveled to Germany with me to perform at a show a friend had organized near where I grew up. I even joined him on stage for an improvised dance. It's amazing how sometimes, simple (yet precious) friendships lead to exceptional projects.

Everything went well. I got to travel for work, training staff in Mexico City, São Paulo, and Miami, and I was in constant communication with all the other offices across Latin America. This was fun and allowed me to work in three languages, which I always appreciate. In the building where we lived, I met another long-term friend, Yaya, an interior decorator. One time, I dropped my keys, and they fell through the elevator shaft, all the way to the basement. I was trapped in the hallway, unable to get into the apartment or leave the building. After waiting for 15 minutes without any neighbors going in or out, I decided to ring her bell. Interestingly, she had an entire box of keys, and one of them opened the service door to our flat. One of Yaya's gifts was extraordinary resourcefulness, which also helped me recuperate my keys later that day – che, ¡qué piola! As I got to know her better, I came to admire her deeply for her hands-on approach to any challenge, a valued trait in any leader.

Apart from work and dance, I spent lots of time exploring the city. I loved the weekend art fair at San Telmo, where two outstanding Tango couples often performed open-air shows to earn a few pesos from onlookers. This is also where I bought one of my favorite paintings – a depiction of a Tango couple by an artist with an eccentric style. Sadly, this painting was later stolen from a storage facility in Brazil because of its silver frame. (I'd gladly have given up the frame to recover that painting, even though they looked perfect together!)

However, in the spring of 2001, the famous monetary crisis hit Argentina, and things started shifting very quickly. Many Argentinians moved to Spain and other places, and the start-up had to cut costs, including for my training and my role. Instead, they asked me to work on a project in the São Paulo office for a couple of months. Although this temporary assignment was less aligned with my passions or strengths, I accepted the challenge. After all, there's always something we can learn, and I didn't have a "next chapter" plan quite yet.

Before that, though, I went on an exhilarating five-week backpacking trip with Martina, my youngest sister. We met up in Cancún, Mexico, from where we took the bus down the coast, stopping at Tulum – which then looked very different to what it is now, with the ruins publicly accessible for anyone, and some huts in the woods, of which we rented one for a night. After this short stop, we took a night bus all the way down through Quintana Roo and Campeche to Chiapas, with our next destination being Palenque, where we arrived at the bus station around 4am. A taxi driver took us to a small pension he recommended, and the sleepy owner let us inside. As soon as we were in our room, we discovered a huge tarantula on the wall. The man had already gone back to sleep, so getting rid of it was on us. I ran into the hallway, where I found a broom, and I chased the tarantula out the window so we could recover from the momentary shock and get a few hours' sleep before venturing out into Palenque and its surroundings, including the mystical Palenque ruins nestled into lavish vegetation – a truly magical place.

After a few days in Palenque, we decided to continue our trip toward Flores in Guatemala. There was no bus to the border, so we took a private service, a car we shared with a few other travelers, to the border, following the instructions of our Lonely Planet book. On our way to the border, we were driving through breathtaking sceneries to the Usumacinta river that marked the border to Guatemala. We crossed the river on a little boat, got our stamp in a small border hut and were now in Guatemala, where we needed to figure out how to continue our expedition to Flores, next to Petén Itzá lake. We enjoyed the relaxing atmosphere next to the lake and some interesting street food, and eventually, we decided (heavyheartedly) to skip picturesque Antigua and take a bus over to San Pedro Sula in Honduras and from there to La Ceiba, as we wanted to get to Roatán Island in time before Easter to make sure we'd still find a nice hut on the beach for ourselves.

After a night in La Ceiba and exploring a nearby beach consisting of beautiful shells of all shapes, colors, and sizes, we took the ferry over to Roatán. This was what I'd remember as one of the two scariest boat rides of my life (the other one being on a fisher boat in Portugal). Even the local commuters were terrified. However, gladly we arrived safely on this paradise island, where we had the most amazing diving experiences you can imagine. Wow, wow, wow!

We decided to get our diving certification on Roatán Island off the northern coast of Honduras, and we certainly did not regret it. Not only did we have amazing and fun diving instructors; this is also the most impressive and colorful diving paradise I've ever seen since. Not that I've been diving much since, but I did experience the underwater world in some places of Brazil, Columbia, and Belize, and I've never seen anything comparable again. If you dive, you must see the underwater beauty of the sea surrounding Roatán!

When it was time to say goodbye, we had spent more time than originally planned, so we decided to take a plane to San José, Costa Rica, the last country in our list for this trip, where we explored places like the Mercado Central and the nearby Jaco Beach and Arenal volcano. I remember the volcano day as the least pleasant of the entire trip: We were really intrigued by it at first. We boarded the bus in a city bathed in bright sunshine, which lasted all the way until we arrived at the foot of the mountain leading up to the volcano, and as we arrived on top, our disappointment was huge as we found the top enveloped in thick, heavy clouds, which never lifted the entire day. But not only that: It had started raining and it actually got also pretty chilly, which we were not prepared for. So, our only option was to wait in the restaurant all day until the bus would pick us up again hours later. I remember us desperately drying our wet socks and sneakers under the bathroom hand dryer. When you don't have lots of options, you use what you have.

Our departure from San José also coincided with my sister and I parting ways at the airport, as she was traveling on to Ecuador and I back to Argentina. She did visit me in Buenos Aires later, though.

Leadership Wisdom – Key Takeaways

Resourcefulness Pays off

Despite the minor setback at the volcano, my trip through Central America left me with cherished memories and precious learnings. Backpacking in times without smartphones or GPS forced me to rely on resourcefulness and creativity. It was a period of discovery, navigating unfamiliar territories, connecting with locals and gaining insights into their lives, while ensuring our safety as tourists. This experience instilled in me the importance of adaptability and thinking outside the box (or throwing the box out altogether), qualities that have proven invaluable in leadership, and really in all my professional endeavors.

Embrace resourcefulness and adaptability in your leadership. Challenge yourself to think creatively and approach obstacles with a fresh perspective. This sometimes requires not just *thinking* outside the box but *stepping* outside the box so you can look at it from the outside and assess if it even still has reason to exist. In some cases, it may be best to throw the entire box out and restart with an entirely new approach.

As part of this process, encourage your team to adopt a creative mindset as well and watch as you all grow stronger and more innovative together.

*

On the plane back to Buenos Aires, I found myself pondering the sacrifices and trade-offs that come with living abroad. Every choice has its bright side and its shadow. While I was deeply grateful for the time spent with my "little" sister on this trip, a part of me ached to see my mom, siblings, and nephews more often, to have those spontaneous moments that distance just doesn't allow, especially with a job tying me down. And I was daydreaming about a future where we could beam ourselves across continents and oceans in the blink of an eye...

Chapter 6

San Francisco Fog and a Turning Point Beneath the Golden Gate

Lessons in Habits and Advocating for Myself

Soon after our Central America trip, while taking care of a temporary assignment in São Paulo, I received an email from the head of the San Francisco office telling me that her job would become available and asking me if I was interested. Given my situation in Buenos Aires, I agreed to job interviews at the San Francisco office. During my visit to San Francisco, I wanted to confirm that the city was right for me, and of course, that I could find some of my then preferred dance options, so I made the best of the few days I had available to get acquainted with the city, including one time getting lost on its many hills.

Long story short, I accepted the job, and we agreed on a start date in November 2001, which gave me enough time to travel back to Munich, get a visa, pack up my things for the move, and cherish a few more months in Munich during an exceptionally warm fall, with many outdoors farewell dinners with friends and lots of dancing.

One night, while out salsa dancing with my friend Manuela, I crossed paths with someone special – a very fun Colombian art dealer and sports reporter, Daniel. We hit it off immediately and had a blast together. However, I knew that he wouldn't be ready to fully commit, and I wasn't about to put my life on hold for someone who wasn't willing to make me number one. Nonetheless, he holds a special place in my heart, and we developed a close friendship – a bond that endured for years, even long after I had moved on. What's astounding is that during my annual visits to Germany in the four years that followed, he always made me a priority.

It was also during this time that I decided to quit smoking. After decades of the habit, kicking it was no small feat. With smoking being banned in one of the Embarcadero Center buildings, where our office was located, the thought of having to trek down the elevator from the 24th floor several times a day for a smoke break while juggling a demanding job was less than appealing. So, I summoned the strength to quit. How did I do it, you might wonder? I convinced myself that I could always smoke "tomorrow." Prohibitions never seemed to work for me, but granting myself permission did. I also employed a little trick: In Munich, where smoking was still quite prevalent at the time, whenever the cravings became overwhelming, I'd indulge in a few puffs of a cigarillo, making a conscious effort not to inhale deeply. Additionally, when out at bars at night, I'd opt for a cigar instead (though not finishing it entirely). It wasn't easy, but after about nine months, I found that I didn't think about it much anymore – except during visits to Germany, where many of my friends still smoked. But I digress; let's get back to the main story!

In November, I found myself back at Munich Airport, ready to hop on a flight and embark on a new adventure that would take me to the West Coast of the United States.

Upon touchdown, I hailed a cab bound for Sansome Street. During the initial weeks, BCG had arranged temporary accommodation near the office in the Financial District, affording me time to hunt for a more permanent residence. Soon, I stumbled upon a colorfully painted floor with a back deck in a Victorian house on Shotwell Street in the Mission district. It wasn't just the warmer climate, the absence of fog, and the abundance of sunshine (San Francisco boasts several micro-climates) that won me over, but also the district's unique *ambiente* and the green and blue kitchen.

From the array of Latino restaurants to the funky stores and bars lining Mission and Valencia Streets, the neighborhood clearly stood out at my best choice. Plus, I loved its proximity to Potrero Hill and Mission Bay, offering some excellent dining options and, most importantly, some of my favorite dancing spots for Thursday nights and weekends, such as Café Cocomo and The Ramp.

An added perk of frequenting Café Cocomo was the attentive bartender who often had his eye on me, resulting in a bounty of complimentary drinks – though, truth be told, I was there primarily for the dancing, usually arriving by car and mindful of the looming workday ahead. Indulging in copious amounts of alcohol wouldn't have been the wisest choice, so I'd limit it to a mimosa or a glass of wine...

Outside of those wild Thursday nights, I soon started taking Flamenco and Afro-Cuban dance at Dance Mission, I refined my Samba no Pé in classes with Mary Dollar's group and my Cuban Salsa with Ramón Ramos, who also became a close friend. We even coordinated a couple of Salsa classes for BCG social events later. But I´m skipping ahead… So let´s start at the beginning:

I found myself back at the SFO office, rehired and ready to dive back into the swing of things.

At the time, I assumed they would be fair with me, offering a competitive salary commensurate with the market. After all, I had dedicated over 12 years of hard work to the company in the past.

However, I neglected to do my due diligence. The salary they offered seemed appealing, especially coming from Argentina – a market with vastly different currency values, lower salary standards, and a much lower cost of living at the time. I failed to make a proper comparison between the two and hastily accepted the offer without negotiating my salary. Truth be told, even if I had done my due diligence, I might still have found that it was up to local standards, although seeing the data might have changed my mindset and led me to negotiate, as it wasn't on the high end of those standards. Live and learn, as they say… And didn't I also under-negotiate my compensation in Munich? Are you seeing a pattern?

About a year later, I stumbled upon a shocking revelation: my counterpart in Los Angeles was making one and a half times my salary! This despite my extensive experience and my role overseeing a considerably larger team and office, and with Los Angeles cost of living being comparable or lower back then. This was information I wasn't meant to uncover, but someone had overlooked deleting her salary from a spreadsheet we used to determine annual raises, and here it was – an unintentional revelation glaring back at me!

I was devastated and requested an adjustment, but it was denied – budgets had been finalized a while back. Instead, my boss assured me she'd put in a word for a higher bonus for the year, only to find out later that it wasn't feasible due to strict bonus regulations, despite her intentions to make up for my disappointment. I was already receiving the highest possible bonus for my staff category, determined by my performance, and the partner group, while recognizing my dedication, didn't want to set a precedence nor would it have been easy to change the overall bonus budget, which had been submitted already. Also, pushing though a 50% raise was understandably not an easy task, and so my salary was never corrected the way it should have been. My only choice for a larger adjustment would have been to take it away from other team members (as our salaries came from the same overall budget), and that was absolutely not something I wanted to do. It was 100% out of question.

Long story short, this experience later strengthened my decision to leave my leader role after 3.5 years in San Francisco, pack up once again and move back to Argentina, this time more permanently with all my belongings.

But before this, I made the best of my stay in San Francisco, touring the beautiful Napa and Sonoma Valleys with their many wineries, the breathtaking drive all the way up to Mendocino, river rafting, the nearby beaches, Tamalpais Park, and forests with giant sequoia trees. I also undertook a couple of hiking trips to Lake Tahoe with friends and drove down on the Pacific Coast Highway to Southern California, visiting places like Santa Cruz, Monterey, Carmel, Big Sur, Los Angeles, and San Diego, and even crossing the Mexican border to visit Tijuana.

On many of these trips, I went with my friend and colleague Beatriz, who was always up for an adventure. One of our trips to Napa Valley landed me at the hospital after kissing a wasp. We'd booked a room in a beautiful bed & breakfast and were enjoying the sunshine in the yard, sipping our coffee as the hosts prepared a savory breakfast with fresh waffles and all. Somehow, a wasp made its way into my cup without me noticing. Though I spit the little bastard out as fast as I could, it managed to sting my tongue. Delicious breakfast, goodbye!

The scariest part was that I wasn't supposed to drive myself, so I had to give Beatriz – who wasn't exactly a manual-shift expert (to say the least!) – a crash course in driving my old Eagle Talon. We managed to get to the emergency room so the dangerous swelling of my tongue could be treated, while both our stomachs loudly lamented the absence of that lavish breakfast. We made up for that hours later with a nice lunch.

Funnily enough, in the summer of 1990, the day before my official start date as a new employee at BCG Munich, I had had an unfortunate encounter with a bee that stung me in the throat, and I'd had to spend several days in the hospital, suffering from the stinging pain long after. Life is full of patterns, isn't it?

With my friend Manuela from my Samba classes in Munich, I rendezvoused in Salvador da Bahia, Brazil, for carnival one year. The Bahia carnival is absolutely wild! It's best not to carry any valuables there; even with the military police relentlessly patrolling the crowds, I still felt strangers' hands in my pockets a few times amidst the crowd. One of the highlights was the contagious *batucadas* in Salvador, along with spectacular performances of several bands.

We also went on a boat trip one day, which was Manuela's birthday present to me, including a diving session. The boat captain inquired if we had taken any medication for seasickness. I proudly claimed I had never been seasick before (plus, I'm not a fan of "prevention meds") – not even on the roughest boat rides or the sailing trip in Spain after partying all night. Little did I anticipate that this time would be different. It reached a point where I couldn't even keep water down! However, I was determined not to waste my diving opportunity. Interestingly, once underwater, the seasickness seemed to dissipate, providing a brief relief despite feeling incredibly weak. By afternoon, we finally returned to shore, utterly famished with empty stomachs! On our way back from the pier, we somehow found ourselves in a posh Italian restaurant amidst elegantly dressed businesspeople finishing late lunches, while we were still in our beachwear and wet bikinis… I was really glad they let us in like that… I could have eaten an entire elephant! Though I settled for a satisfying seafood pasta dish.

Later, we made our way up the coast to other carnival-celebrating towns, such as Maceió, Recife and Olinda, where the sounds of Frevo filled the streets. We also visited the nearby Porto de Galinhas, renowned for its exceptional snorkeling. Of course, we had to confirm this reputation through our own experience! As a Pisces, I've always felt a deep, magnetic pull from the ocean. Fish love water, don't they?

On another trip from San Francisco, I flew down to Belize, landing in Belize City. From there, I took a bus down the coast to Garifuna towns like Dadringa, where I stayed for a night, and finally reached Placencia, where I rented one of three beachfront huts. At first, I wasn't aware that I was going to be the only one staying on that small stretch of beach. At night, with only the sound of ocean waves and the shadows of the palm trees dancing on the roof, it was both beautiful and a bit eerie being alone there, so I decided to move to a room in a house in town.

With just nine days in total, my plans to dive were thwarted by a recent hurricane that had devastated underwater areas, leaving strong winds in its wake. Despite this, I managed to fit in one dive towards the end of my trip. After enduring a very bumpy boat ride to a distant sandbank, where the other passengers stayed for snorkeling, the dive instructor and I ventured further into the murky waters. Although the hurricane had clouded the water and obscured much of the underwater beauty, I distinctly remember the dive instructor placing a huge black water spider on the back of my hand – that was a first, and an unforgettable one! Another highlight was befriending the owner of the local dive shop, who later took me Punta dancing at a bar. Connecting with locals always enriches the travel experience, offering genuine insights into their way of life.

Back in San Francisco, I immersed myself in Shamanic Studies and later added some basic Reiki to my repertoire. Every week, I'd drive to Shaman Isa's place to join other students in Shamanic Journeying and related healing sessions. This was the start of a long discovery of holistic studies. Though this was briefly interrupted by my next destination, I eventually picked it back up in Brazil.

My stay in the San Francisco melting pot was also marked by three romantic relationships with men from three different cultures – Jamaica, Cameroon, and Nicaragua, one of which left a deep mark on my life, while all three provided profound opportunities for my personal growth. The one that stands out is with my Cameroonian boyfriend Olivier, who literally seemed to have resurfaced from a previous life… Have you ever experienced this? You meet someone, and it's as if you'd known them forever. This is not the only time this has happened to me. It's happened multiple times! When you know, you know… André, the Jamaican architect, also had a special place in my heart. In fact, I stayed in contact with both for years and we'd sometimes meet when I traveled back to San Fran to take care of paperwork related to my re-entry permit. (I wanted to keep my green card, which turned out to be a smart move – thanks to my intuition's nudge, given that I chose New York City as my neew home seven years after leaving the U.S. for Latin America).

On one of my trips back to Europe, my sister Rosmarie and her little son Moritz joined me on a spontaneous adventure to Crete. We rented a car to explore the island, and the soundtrack for our excursions came from Moritz, who turned every object he found into an instrument, filling the car with his playful music and sweet singing. It had been ages since I'd traveled around Europe, and this was my first time setting foot in Greece – a culture I only knew from the stories of a friend who'd been traveling there regularly, as well as the many Greek restaurants in Germany. One day, we ventured into the mountains, following what seemed like a scenic route leading to a viewpoint. But when we hit a dead end, our tiny car struggled to turn around. There was no one nearby, and we definitely didn't want to spend the night there. Gladly, we eventually managed to maneuver our way out… Every twist and turn of the road literally promised something unexpected in those mountains.

Back in San Francisco, for my 40th birthday, I threw a big party. My landlord had just vacated the floor below mine, and he generously let me use the entire empty space to fit everyone in. I prepared a huge spread of finger food, including some intricate delicacies, and we danced Salsa, Samba, and Tango until our feet couldn't take it anymore. It was also the first warm day of the season, so we enjoyed the back deck as well. We all had an amazing time. I hadn't thrown many big birthday parties in my life, so this one was truly special.

But despite my eventful time there and the appealing sceneries of the nearby coastline, San Francisco never quite felt like home to me as much as other places did, and I also craved a warmer climate. On top of that, my salary experience left a bad taste in my mouth. Meanwhile, Buenos Aires was calling me back, stirring up nostalgia from the south – probably because my soul still sensed some unfinished business there.

Besides, I was ready for something new and exciting! I had a vision of opening a bed & breakfast tailored for Tango enthusiasts, so I decided to take the plunge and make it a reality. I sold my old Mitsubishi Eagle Talon, packed up my belongings, and arranged for them to be shipped down the coast to Argentina in the deep south. And so, my chapter in San Francisco came to a close.

In reflecting on this chapter of my life, two profound lessons emerge: the transformative power of changing habits and the imperative need to advocate for myself and negotiate powerfully.

Leadership Wisdom – Key Takeaways

Change Your Habits, Change Your Life

The journey of breaking the shackles of smoking was both arduous and immensely rewarding. The decision to quit, though initially daunting, proved invaluable. Beyond reclaiming precious time from otherwise unavoidable smoke breaks, the benefits transcended mere convenience. Adopting a smoke-free lifestyle not only revitalized my physical well-being but made dancing with me a more pleasant experience for my dance partners. You could say the investment in this change paid long-term dividends.

The initial phase was the opposite of what I'd expected: I coughed a lot, gained weight, and felt more sluggish and less energized due to the physical changes and processing. But I'm glad I persevered, and I've never touched a cigarette again.

Even if you've never been a smoker, I hope my example inspires you to challenge some other limiting habit you've identified in yourself. Are you procrastinating on an important project? Making excuses to avoid starting? Or perhaps you're addicted to your devices or gaming? Do you consume too much junk food or still drink those unhealthy sodas? (A little tip: Researching the ingredients in some popular brands might motivate you to avoid them.)

Here's the thing with habits: They are sticky. Why? – Because our brains love sameness and the habitual. They take shortcuts in thinking and avoid what they perceive as risk, automatically reverting to the known rather than urging us to step into the unknown. Your habit is part of your conditioning, keeping you on autopilot. When you break the pattern, your body sounds the alarm, convincing you it's unsafe to change. You start saying things like, "I'll do it tomorrow." Your body knows you're lying, so it calms down.

Don't put it off! The longer you wait, the harder it becomes because habits only get stickier with time. The best time for change is *now*. When you change your habits, you change your life.

Advocating for Myself

I was forced to confront the sobering reality of undervaluing my worth, particularly in salary negotiations. This pattern of self-underestimation, recurring like a stubborn echo, demanded my attention. Quantified in financial terms, not negotiating my salary resulted in a huge cost: a staggering loss of nearly $300,000 over a mere three years, compounded by missing contributions to my pension fund during two years of my tenure in Germany.

This painful lesson underscored the urgent need to break free from this detrimental cycle; to assertively own the value I bring to the table; and champion for myself and rightful compensation. It inspired me to dig deep into this topic, address the beliefs and thought patterns that had kept the pattern in place for too long, and transform my mindset in a way that I can now teach it to my clients.

To everyone else, it serves as a poignant reminder of the transformative potential inherent in breaking patterns, upleveling our mindset, and asserting our worth, paving the way for a future defined by self-empowerment.

Do you know you should be earning more than you currently are? Do you deserve a bigger paycheck than you're taking home each month? Then it's time to negotiate! Don't delay; it won't get easier later!

If you're applying for a new job and are afraid that asking for the salary you truly want might lead to rejection, remember this: if you're truly an ideal candidate for the role, you can often negotiate better than what's initially offered. When asked about your salary expectations, always start higher than what you actually want. You can negotiate down, but it's nearly impossible to negotiate up once a number has been stated, and you might be surprised to get more than you expected. Plus, it's usually much harder to renegotiate salary later.

Salary negotiations are not the time for people-pleasing. In fact, people-pleasing and prioritizing others' approval over your own needs is counterproductive in most situations, as it often means putting yourself last. This approach not only undermines your own interests but can also harm the quality of your relationship with your manager. To achieve a fair outcome and avoid resentment, disappointment, or other feelings that might affect the relationship, it's essential to advocate for yourself confidently and assertively.

If you are still unsure how to position the value you bring to your job and how to effectively negotiate the compensation you deserve, check out my Dream Salary Course. It teaches you the mindset and essential steps needed to prepare for and successfully navigate a salary negotiation.

*

On my way to the airport, as I was looking out the windows of my cab, a movie of all the wonderful experiences in this Far West city was playing in my mind. Only three and a half years, and so much had happened! One of the experiences is too intimate and delicate to share it here. But it would sure touch me on a deep level and change some of my convictions going forward. It was a bitter-sweet goodbye. I was leaving behind one of the big loves of my life and dear friends, like Julia, André, Olivier, Beatriz, Ramón, Stefan, Corrie, María, Rick, José, Marija, Nii-Akanu, Katy, Tom, Vicky, my downstairs neighbors, and many others. I realized I sure had a lot of friends there and I would miss them.

Chapter 7

Walking through Buenos Aires with Hundreds of Thousands in My Socks

Lessons in Perseverance, Visioning, and Service

V ámonos de garufa – let's have some fun – in Buenos Aires! *Garufa* is a Lunfardo word, it's the title of a Tango, and it was also the name I gave my first entrepreneurial venture. It means "boisterous fun," usually relating to a night out dancing Tango. But more about that in a bit! First things first...

In 2005, I moved from San Francisco to Buenos Aires to open a bed & breakfast with an investor's visa and a dream in my pocket.

To turn this dream into a physical reality, I needed cash, meaning I had to transfer my savings to Argentina. To avoid the hassle and expense of exchanging currency twice – from USD to Argentine pesos and back to USD to buy a property – I opted for a more unconventional route, one often used by the wealthy but less known to the general public.

A friend in Argentina introduced me to someone in the money transfer business. However, the transfer hit a snag. Days turned into weeks, and my money still hadn't arrived. Anxiety set in as I waited and waited, with my entire savings on the line.

At the time, I was also working as an external consultant at the Buenos Aires BCG office, going in once a week and even also traveling to Santiago de Chile to mentor staff there. One day, after my regular work hours, I stayed late to use the office internet to track down my missing funds. (I didn't have internet at home yet, as I was still setting up my house.)

In an almost miraculous turn of events, I found my money online. It didn't take long, and I can't recall exactly how I found the right place to search. It felt like a little voice guided me there – intuition or perhaps a spirit guide. Ever had that experience? Like someone's whispering in your ear or pointing you to turn your focus to a specific spot? It turned out the money was stuck en route due to a lack of proper instructions for its final destination. There had been a hiccup in the process!

This money represented all my savings, except for a smaller amount I had sent through a different channel to meet the requirements for my investor's visa. The whole experience was a nightmare. I kept thinking, what if all my money was lost?

Can you imagine the relief when I found it? No more sleepless nights. Now it was only a matter of a couple more days for the entire process to be completed. First hurdle taken!

The next step in my plan was to find the perfect property for my B&B project. A former colleague's architect friend had spotted a place that seemed to meet my requirements. This was how after a surprisingly short search, I discovered a house in Palermo Hollywood, right in the heart of a bustling restaurant district. It was the ideal location, and with some remodeling, it would be perfect for my purposes.

Buying the house turned out to be far more adventurous than I had anticipated. The transaction required a cash payment, and the reality of this hit home as I found myself sitting in a bank's meeting room, literally counting out the dollars. To make this happen, I first had to transport my cash to the seller's bank. Without a car and having been warned against taking a cab due to the high risk of robbery (there had been incidents with taxi drivers targeting customers carrying large sums to and from banks), I faced a daunting challenge.

So, on a sweltering summer day in Buenos Aires, I found myself carrying several hundred thousand dollars across the city, hidden in my socks. Every step was fraught with tension – one wrong move, and all my savings could have been gone! Savings I had worked over 15 years to accumulate. This nerve-wracking experience taught me a valuable lesson: when you want something really bad, sometimes you have to take a risk.

The buildout took longer than expected due to the major changes I had requested: converting a small swimming pool into a deck, transforming the garage into a kitchen, and a complete remodel of the house. This included installing air conditioning, adding three bathrooms, painting every inch inside and out, and furnishing it with unique pieces. I sourced most of the furniture from auctions in the suburbs, combining these finds with my existing pieces that were arriving with my move. It was a joy to transform this traditional casa de salchicha (or "sausage house" due to its typical shape) into a vibrant, colorful retreat. The house ended up looking like a lively Mexican guest house, with each room and bathroom showcasing two dominant colors. Even the bathroom tiles were artisanal masterpieces from a local tile manufacturer.

I was thrilled with the final result. To manage the guest rooms and prepare daily breakfasts, I hired a housekeeper. We opened the bed and breakfast within 12 months, just in time to meet the investor's visa requirements: open a business and create at least one job. Despite the challenge of manual labor and minimal machinery, I made it happen! Yay!

I threw a huge party for pretty much everyone I knew in Buenos Aires: from the architect and contractor who helped with the remodel to my dancer friends from the Tango and Brazilian Zouk scenes, old colleagues, and even my ex-neighbor Yaya from my previous stay. We had a full house. I served homemade *empanadas*, Argentinian wine flowed freely, and, of course, dancing was a central part of the celebration.

One of my strategies was to email all B&B guests with a link to leave a review, and thanks to the delicious breakfast with home-made bread, the luxurious rest on top-quality mattresses, and our excellent customer service, including insider tips off the beaten track, Garufa quickly climbed to the #1 spot on TripAdvisor and maintained that position nearly the entire time it was open. Garufa was also featured in *Hoteles*, a high-end hotel magazine, as well as in *Lonely Planet* and several other travel guides.

The only fact that overshadowed the situation was that I still hadn't obtained my business license. Now, I could not have put off the opening because that would have meant losing my investor's visa, which came with some strings attached, including a launch date within 12 months and hiring at least one employee.

This meant I couldn't possibly comply with the requirements of all the agencies, with one asking me to open and the other requiring me to have a license to open. The famous conundrum of the snake that bites its own tail... Little did I know that some (most?) of the other B&Bs didn't have licenses either!

I never received that license, and neither did many others. It seemed like they did it on purpose. I applied for the license as soon as I had the plans from the architect. The agency charged me for it, but never actually granted it. There was nothing fundamentally wrong with the plans; they just required a few minor initial changes, which I included in the remodeling process.

As I later found out through the grapevine, the public "authorities" did the same thing with other B&Bs, too. It was their way of setting the scene to collect bribes,... lots of money under the table, again and again... Inspectors would show up at the B&B and say, "Oh, you don't have a license..." I never let them inside.

Eventually, I discovered a way around needing a license, so I beat them with their own weapons: If I only advertised three rooms total, I'd be fine. The inspectors still showed up, but I never opened the door for them; just told them they didn't have the right to enter. And that's how I got fined. But it didn't end here...

I went to the city hall and spoke to their supervisor, who insisted I should just pay the fine. I refused and I decided to contest it. The case went to court. On the day of the trial, one of the inspectors was called as a witness. He pretended not to remember what happened, but when the judge asked me to describe the incident, I hinted at corruption. The moment the judge heard the word "corrupt," she was all ears. "Tell me more!" she said.

In the end, the verdict was in my favor. I won the case, thanks to the right judge at the right time. However, no one covered my legal expenses. My lawyer, who did little to prepare for the trial, was too complacent due to the frequent cases he handled and that he made tons of money with.

What mattered most to me was that I didn't have to pay the fine and that I stood up for myself against corrupt "authorities," rather than taking the easier route of bowing down. And I managed to do it in court all by myself, without even knowing what to expect and without any help from my lazy lawyer.

Before we dive into more pleasant topics in the next chapter, let's quickly recap the key points.

Leadership Wisdom – Key Takeaways

Perseverance Pays Off

Looking back on those tumultuous days, I am reminded of the power of perseverance – the unwavering belief that with enough determination and grit, even the most daunting challenges can be conquered. My time in Buenos Aires was more than just a chapter in my life; it was a testament to the indomitable spirit of the human soul, a journey of self-discovery and transformation, and a preparation for the next challenge ahead... because we can find corruption all over the world, and sure as hell, I did in my capacity as a business owner in Brazil. I believe these challenges also prepared me for the intense times that started in 2020; they gave me strength, because while I'm not a fan of negativity at all, there is some truth to the saying "What doesn't kill you makes you stronger."

Visionary Leaders Need Dreams Because… Dreams Become Visions

Visionary leaders are dreamers and risk-takers. Those dreams become their visions. For them to implement their visions, they need to be prepared to experiment with new ways of doing, try new things.

I've often heard: "Dreams don't come true. Plans do." But there are no big plans without big dreams. We turn our dreams into visions, which we then set goals and make a plan for; the vision serving us as our GPS and the goals being our milestones along the way.

Create your own powerful vision and let it guide you. It's ok to become creative even in areas that you don't feel 100% prepared for, like I did when I created my own Tango show, telling a story on stage; or when I started my first business. – I had no prior experience in the hospitality sector except as a customer. I learned by doing, as has been the case with many other professional activities I've successfully carried out over the years. And there are always experts you can turn to or hire for help, advice or coaching.

Excellent Service Brings More Customers

Distinguishing myself through excellent service clearly paid off for me as a B&B owner. I made it easy for my guests to have a pleasant time while in Buenos Aires, and I even advised them for their travels to other parts of the country, as I had traveled myself extensively, and mostly by bus, meaning, I had acquired solid knowledge about each region and climate that helped my customers find the options that were right for them.

This service spanned from the booking experience (making it easy to find me through TripAdvisor and offering a website in five languages), taking payments in three currencies, offering tourist information off the beaten track making their stay special in this way, getting them tickets to the best Tango show package (great venue, show, and food), delicious breakfast, appealing atmosphere and convenient link to the review, which wouldn't take them more than three minutes to complete. They got the full package. I still keep the guest book with all the appreciative comments in it…

*

Ok, now, as promised, let me tell you about the fun stuff…

Chapter 8
Passion and Spotlight: Tango, Movies, and Friendships

Lessons in Stepping Outside the Box

Shortly after moving to Buenos Aires, I had met Ana María, who'd become my closest friend and who'd accompany me through thick and thin. I would sometimes cook – Ana María adored my spicy shrimp curries and my Italian dishes – and we'd sit at my large, rustic dining table talking for hours and hours. Ana María later introduced me to Marcela, who often had us over to her house for sumptuous meals with her entire family. Those became some unforgettable moments for me that I'm immensely grateful for. My friendship with Ana María lasted well beyond my time in Argentina, and we still occasionally check in on each other. She remains a key member of my core group of friends scattered across the planet – those individuals I feel I was destined to meet for profound reasons. There was simply no way around it.

Since I had a big open-air space with a built-in barbecue on the upper floor, I often invited friends over for a traditional *asado* (barbecue). We'd grill, dance, and hang out, usually on Sunday afternoons when the B&B guests were out sightseeing. Everyone loved coming by, and I didn't mind spending the rest of the evening washing dishes afterward – those gatherings were always worth it!

My neighbor, Norma, who ran a casting company, and I had also become good friends. This is how I had the unique opportunity to play extra roles in two notable movies, *Negro Buenos Aires* and *The City of Your Final Destination*. Norma graciously extended invitations to participate when suitable opportunities arose, such as when they required Tango dancers for a scene. It was a great experience to not just be in front of a camera but also experience what was going on behind the scenes.

Once, I had to undergo minor surgery on my foot to remove a malignant spot. Since dancing (especially in high heels) and walking were not recommended, I decided to make the best of the situation. I packed a bag and went straight from the doctor's office to the bus station, taking a roughly 12-hour ride to Mendoza, renowned for its excellent wines and beautiful historic wineries. While there, I took several day trips on local buses around the region, and I paid a two-day visit to San Juan. I figured limited walking was ok… and it sure was.

As you can see, I always find a way to stay on the move, although, admittedly, it became more challenging the day I sprained my ankle… But even then, I was hopping up and down the stairs in the house on one leg and back on the dance floor soon after, sporting a supportive bandage, just without the heels.

One of the most memorable highlights during my time in Buenos Aires was the Tango show we created ourselves. Our Tango instructors Ernesto and Norma initiated a project where each of us had the opportunity to craft and direct our own Tango performance, complete with a storyline of our own creation. We all took part in each other's shows, which were showcased as part of a public event organized by our instructors. For my show, I decided to tell a story through the dancing legs of a Tango couple, and it turned out amazing! I used a curtain that covered the dancers' bodies from the knees up, so the audience would only see their lower legs. (I'm still a little proud of that idea.)

Witnessing my own concept, screenplay, and direction come to life on stage on the day of the show was truly gratifying, and I was delighted to contribute to the success of my fellow students' productions as well. We all danced in each other's shows – a wonderful experience!

Tango nights always began late. I'd typically head out around 10:30 or 11pm, but most people wouldn't show up until midnight. There was even an after-hours milonga in Palermo Viejo that we'd flock to when the other milongas closed around 4am.

The Tango scene is a science unto itself, rich with rules and traditions. One such tradition is the *cabeceo* – subtle eye contact often paired with a small nod. This can easily be misinterpreted, leading to awkward moments, like standing up only to realize the nod was meant for someone else – yikes, how embarrassing! When the follower doesn't want to dance, she simply won't respond to his eye contact. If she does respond, the leader typically approaches her table to invite her to dance (traditionally, the follower is female and the leader male, though this can, of course, vary).

Cortinas are short pieces of music in between *tandas* sets of three to five songs). They signal dancers to return to their seats and clear the floor. Etiquette dictates that you dance with the same partner until the end of the *tanda,* which can be delightful, painful, or anything in between. In more traditional Tango settings, it is considered unacceptable for a follower to leave the dance floor before the end of a *tanda*, especially if she is not among the top 5%-ranked dancers. Doing so can have significant social repercussions and may even affect her standing within the Tango community. The *Tango Nuevo* scene, on the other hand, tends to be more forgiving as the rules are more relaxed, and traditions not as strictly followed.

There is a wealth of books that describe Tango traditions. Over the years, I translated ten books on Argentine Tango as well as the culture of *yerba mate* tea to German for Abrazos, a publishing house owned by my friend Daniel Canuti. This experience taught me a great deal about the history of Tango and Lunfardo, the slang of Buenos Aires and the Tango culture. Lunfardo, an argot that includes lots of words with Italian roots as well as *vesre* (word mashups, from "revés" or "al revés," which means "upside down" or "the other way around"), is prominent in Tango lyrics. After translating numerous Tango lyrics for a book about Carlos Gardel, as well as other volumes, I became quite adept at understanding and using Lunfardo.

In Buenos Aires, my dance repertoire extended beyond Tango and Milonga. I also deepened my Brazilian Zouk skills with my friend Claudio (even though that dance was never gonna be my strong suit –

my body is just not made for it), and later, I ventured into learning Samba de Gafieira. This newfound passion for Samba de Gafieira even led me to undertake short trips to Rio de Janeiro for further training and practice, with my first classes being with Rodrigo Marques and Carol Vilanova. Look them up online! They are true stars, and you will get a wonderful taste of this intricate dance.

These experiences sparked a profound affection for Rio de Janeiro, a city I had previously only glimpsed during brief visits lasting no more than a day or two. And that's what eventually led to a brand-new chapter in my life… but before then, I still had to sell my house in Palermo and organize my move… not the last one in my life for sure.

This is remarkable because I once believed I might stay in Buenos Aires indefinitely, if not forever. Interestingly, it wouldn't be the last time I had such thoughts about a place.

Leadership Wisdom – Key Takeaways

Stepping Outside Our Usual Field of Action Broadens Our Horizon

Exploring new ventures beyond our usual field of expertise not only enriches our lives but also expands our perspectives. Whether it's writing and directing a Tango show, stepping in front of the camera as an extra for a movie, or translating Tango lyrics from Lunfardo, these experiences allowed me to discover hidden talents and find new excitement. They reminded me that growth often lies outside our "known zone," offering fresh insights and new connections. Specifically, the staging of a Tango show inspired me to trust my creativity and explore the role of a director/choreographer, which I'd never thought I'd ever be in.

It can be tremendously refreshing to embrace the unknown. There's always a world of opportunity on the other side. Do you feel stuck or bored in any way? Try something new! Get out of your routine and see where the adventure takes you. The unknown is filled with surprises!

Start by making a short list of things you've always wanted to do and pick one to start with… now!

*

As I was boarding the plane at my departure from the grand city of Buenos Aires, I was filled with a sense of gratitude – for the challenges overcome, the lessons learned, and the dreams realized. But also for the many dear friends I'd made there: Ana Maria, Claudio, Gianna, Mario, Yaya, Mónica, Marcela, Alejandra, Vale, Norma, Ernesto, Omar, Eduardo, Alejandro, Alberto, Mariano, Miguel, Oscar, Jorge, Lucas, Gonzalo, Laura, Dani, Adriano, and many more… Saying goodbye is always the hardest part.

And as I hopped into the next chapter of my journey called life, I carried with me the enduring wisdom gleaned from my time in Argentina – the knowledge that with courage and determination, anything is possible.

Chapter 9
Rio de Janeiro – Dancing Through Heaven and Hell

*Lessons in Self-Empowerment, Self-Forgiveness,
Deliberate Choices, and Resilience*

During the first year in Rio de Janeiro, I thought I'd never leave this wickedly beautiful place. It felt as if I'd fallen out of an airplane right onto cloud nine. I loved its tropical climate and lush vegetation, the ocean with its large, beautiful beaches right next to me, and the rain forest with its trails and waterfalls intertwined with the city. The hills, like the Sugar Loaf, offered breathtaking views. The vibrant culture, filled with Samba and other dances, captivated me. Paragliding in São Conrado, though I only experienced it much later, was the icing on the cake.

The indescribable beauty of Rio is forever imprinted in my memory in its many colors, despite its many shadows, such as the high crime rates and favelas controlled by drugs and gangs… and my own experience with my fraudulent business partner, all of which also turned my time in Rio into one of endless lessons and as a result, humongous growth. But let me start from the beginning…

In late 2008, when I arrived in Rio de Janeiro, ready for a new life, I was euphoric at the prospect of my next project, even though its exact form had yet to crystallize in my mind.

I remember clearly sitting atop the sturdy Arpoador boulder, strategically placed between Copacabana and Ipanema beaches, which were glittering in the evening sun. As I gazed across the ocean and the bustling beaches in both directions, a profound realization dawned on me: This is my new home! My heart swelled with joy and excitement. Tudo jóia!

I've always appreciated the sensation of arriving in a new place, ready for a fresh adventure, eager to grab its opportunities while anticipating the inevitable twists and turns that life brings. But this was special: It was majestic.

Gradually, I was gaining clarity on what business to launch next. I wanted its core to be about dance, possibly even dance therapy. However, I didn't really have any dance therapy background, and I didn't just want to be the administrator of the place, so after a while, I pivoted to "dance and wellness studio."

By now, it's probably clear where the "dance" aspect of the new business came from, isn't it? I included the wellness component for three reasons: First, I had started studying BodyTalk and later added ThetaHealing, Reconnective Healing, and other modalities to my holistic repertoire. Second, although I loved dancing, I wasn't at a teaching level and wanted to actively participate in the offered activities. Finally, I aimed to provide yoga, Pilates sessions, and massage therapy. Hence, the "wellness."

I explored several potential locations for the business, once again armed with an investor's visa that required me to make an investment within a specific timeframe. Meanwhile, I began taking Samba de Gafieira classes with a dance instructor who later became my – spoiler alert – (fraudulent) business partner. I choose not to disclose his name here, as this book isn't about pointing fingers; it's about sharing lessons learned. Karma has its own way of dealing with things, and it can sure be a bitch. So, let's call him X. But first things first:

I found a beautiful, spacious apartment with a huge balcony in the Flamengo Beach area, and it was love at first sight. Although it was too large for me, I was expecting my belongings from Argentina and had kept a lot of furniture from the B&B that I had acquired with such dedication from auctions and other places. The owner of the apartment required me to either pay for a very expensive insurance policy or have a guarantor who owned at least two properties. I made a deal with X, who was looking to pay off the mortgage for a small apartment. We agreed that I would prepay a series of one-on-one classes with him, which I planned to take anyway, benefiting us both. I got the apartment and moved in, and I absolutely loved it! It was just a few blocks from Flamengo Park and the beach, conveniently located next to the subway. My living room had a lovely view of a green hill with a favela on top, across from a quiet street. There was an amazing tree by my bedroom window, exuding a rich fragrance while it bloomed. Sometimes, I even slept on my garden lounger on the balcony.

One day, while strolling through the Tijuca neighborhood, I discovered what seemed like the perfect house for my business. It was a small schoolhouse that was for sale, needing some repairs and a fresh coat of paint, but it was exactly right for my project. It also aligned with X's plans to expand his presence into this neighborhood, in addition to his other studio. The Universe seemed to have placed it right in my path.

I bought the place and hired a contractor, a friend of X's. It soon became clear that the job was too big for him. He cut corners with cheap materials, and one day, toward the end of the buildout, a painter showed up with a gun at the construction site because the contractor hadn't paid him. With serious flaws emerging, I had to borrow money from family and friends to hire a second contractor who could fix the installations with better materials. In Brazil, I had to pay everything in cash – from the property to the remodeling to the furniture – just like I had done in Argentina. Eventually, the place was finished, its bright green façade gleaming in the sunshine. I hired staff for cleaning and reception, and we geared up for inauguration day. Karla da Silva, a musician friend, whose music I frequently danced to in the *casas de samba* in Lapa, agreed to bring her band for free as an inauguration gift.

Meanwhile, X and I had our eyes on another project in Lapa, a *casa de samba* we considered turning into a restaurant with dancing. It seemed like a golden opportunity, but it quickly soured. After I signed a contract with X and deposited money into a joint account, the third partner made exorbitant demands, causing the project to fall apart. When I tried to retrieve my money, I discovered X had taken a large sum to buy a new car. Shocked and betrayed, I asked him to get a loan and repay me, but he refused, citing high costs. This led to a huge conflict, affecting our other business and the prepaid dance classes. Working – or even dancing – with someone who embezzled money from me felt impossible. Additionally, I had paid him for the use of his brand, which was crucial for gaining traction in my business, as without his name, a new samba dance studio would have faced too much established competition in a city like Rio de Janeiro.

I faced a triple loss: the prepaid dance classes, the brand fee I had paid, and a business that would be much harder to manage and generate profit with… all that with the inauguration approaching fast. Complicating matters further, I had to deal with local Evangelicals targeting me because of the name I ingenuously chose for the wellness part of the business, Yemanjá, the Afro-Brazilian goddess of the sea. I had favored this name because to me, she was a symbol for the ocean. Rio's proximity to the sea, which I loved, and my zodiac sign, Pisces, made it meaningful to me. And so it was that I found dead pigeons in my yard, thrown by people who ironically used candomblé practices against me, while officially condemning anything related to African-rooted gods. So much for "holiness…"

To top it off, we had bats in the trees in front of the house. Just days after painting the façade bright green, it was covered in brown spots from bat droppings, as was the entrance and yard. I wanted to cry. The stains never came off the façade, and we had to brush the floors daily for months before and after opening, despite installing special lights to deter the bats. Cleaning up bat droppings was the last thing I wanted to do.

Overall, it was a rough start after investing all my savings and over a year of work into this brick-and-mortar business, not to mention dealing with the nightmare bureaucracy and condescending civil servants who expected bribes (which I never paid). We had the opening party anyway, with fewer attendees than planned due to X's lack of promotion. I made the best of it, performing a Bolero showcase with a dancer friend, Leo, and spent the rest of the evening dancing Samba and Forró.

I tried to keep the business going, doing my best to attract customers, but they were scarce. I had some regulars for Pilates, for which I'd invested in a range of equipment, as well as for yoga, and a small group faithfully attended the dance classes.

Meanwhile, I immersed myself in Samba de Gafieira with incredibly talented dancers and instructors, primarily with Hugo Roberto, and occasionally with Rodrigo Marques, Leo Fortes, Flávio Marques, and Ana Paula Pereira. (Look them up on YouTube – they are fabulous dancers!) These classes kept me feeling alive and motivated. Early morning walks along the still deserted Flamengo Beach provided some peace. My friend Miriam from São Paulo often stayed at my place while working in Rio, and later I sublet a few rooms to bring in extra income. I also started doing more translations again.

However, I eventually had to face the sobering truth: the costs to maintain the place were unsustainable. Reluctantly, I decided to close the business and sell everything I'd bought for it – furniture, equipment, everything – for a fraction of its value. Selling the house presented another challenge because documentation issues that hadn't surfaced when I bought it now came to light. This dragged out the sale for months, incurring additional expenses.

It felt like my entire world was falling apart. The "should-haves" incessantly swirled through my mind, shattering my self-esteem and plummeting my confidence. I will never forget that feeling. For a while, I avoided dancing in public, fearing everyone knew how "naive and stupid" I had been. Eventually, I returned to the dance floor and resumed my classes with Hugo, but my life in Rio was never the same.

Dealing with public agencies to sort the house papers and trying to sell it felt like torture. At one point, I even had to hire a lawyer to contest a ridiculously high water bill imposed by the utilities company's corrupt staff – a fraudulent practice affecting many others, as I later discovered. It was not an easy time. Can you feel me?

I decided to sue X to seek justice. I hired three different lawyers for the three claims, one of whom turned out to be a fraud, though I discovered that much later. Two cases were won, but by the time the judgments came through, I had already moved to New York City. The Brazilian real had lost value against the U.S. dollar, and I also had to pay the lawyers a percentage. The third case is still stuck in the "justice" system, and that particular lawyer stopped answering my calls. He was probably bought off by my adversary. Overall, it was a significant monetary loss.

This entire experience spanning over several years was extremely painful. However, I don't consider it a waste of time. At its core, nothing really is. Every single situation and everyone we encounter as we move along in life teaches us something. This ordeal was no exception. It taught me valuable lessons, which I will share at the end of this chapter. And... without this experience, I likely wouldn't be doing what I do today. And I had my wonderful friends Sabrina, Ahmyna, Luciana, Patricia, Raquel, Hugo, Adriano, Miriam, Daisy, Fábio, Giselle, Cris, and many more.

During this tumultuous time, I became severely ill with dengue fever. I managed the symptoms for months using holistic healing techniques I had learned. However, given that it was also a time of considerable stress, the illness worsened to the point where I could only eat fruit. Even vegetables made me feel sick just by looking at them, and my skin started to turn red. This happened during a ThetaHealing seminar I was attending. The group performed a healing on me, which provided temporary relief.

About a week later, still with reddish skin, my friend Miriam urged me to get checked at a nearby hospital. They discovered I had hardly any blood left in my veins, making the blood test quite torturous. The diagnosis was dengue fever. They admitted me immediately, rehydrating me through a drip. Within a few days, I was stable enough to return home. I requested to be discharged at my own risk because I wanted to be in the familiar environment of my home, though my single hospital room was quite comfortable, and the food was decent. This experience was in stark contrast to my later hospitalization in New York for malaria, but more about that in a later chapter.

Throughout all this turmoil, I continued my holistic studies, which proved to be a tremendous blessing. I met wonderful friends like Sabrina and Ahmyna, who stood by my side during those challenging times. Holistic healing literally saved me. Understanding the subconscious mind and what drives our patterns, coupled with sessions generously offered by my new friends, helped me move out of victim mode and into a self-empowering mindset. I also started working on my energy, rebuilding my self-esteem, and forgiving myself – the hardest part. It was much easier to forgive my fraudulent "friend" and business partner than it was to forgive myself. Have you ever experienced this?

Transformation is rarely a sudden phenomenon; it unfolds gradually, much like an alchemical process that demands time and patience. It took me a while to recognize the blessing in this experience: it taught me profound lessons, mainly the importance of taking full responsibility – not just for what had happened in this case, but for my entire life. I shifted away from a victim mindset towards a self-empowering one, and I realized that 100% responsibility for our experiences leads to 100% freedom, even though I'm not claiming that I've mastered the full depth of this insight in practical terms quite yet… Still working on it every day, though, which is what matters. Progress rather than perfection.

From then on, my life took on a whole new trajectory. Operating from a self-empowered perspective means understanding that setbacks are temporary, and resilience resides within us. A self-empowering mindset brings the insight that when we fall, we can always get back up. We just need to connect with this enormous power inside us.

This realization fueled my decision to coach others to embrace their own power. As we navigate life's lessons, we are presented with endless chances to evolve and create something even greater. Or, as I like to say: "When life gives you lemons, make a whiskey sour (or, if you happen to be in Brazil, perhaps a caipirinha)."

While I usually favor a nice glass of wine (and lots of water in hot climates!), in Brazil, caipirinhas and beer are the preferred dinner companions for non-teetotalers. During my time in Rio, I enjoyed my fair share of "caipis," with my favorite being the passionfruit variation – always without sugar, as I can't stand sugary drinks. Caipirinha is made with sugarcane schnapps called *cachaça* or *pinga*.

There's a picturesque village halfway between Rio and São Paulo called Paraty, famous for its large selection of *cachaça* and its charming pedestrian-only cobblestone streets lined with white houses featuring colorfully painted doors and windows. Paraty is renowned for producing some of the best *cachaça* in all of Brazil, and visitors can sample a wide variety of these strong, tasty brews – at least as many as they can handle!

Among my visits to other places like Porto Seguro (for dancing Lambada Zouk and Axé), nearby Angra dos Reis, Cabo Frio, and Búzios, Itacaré stood out to me. Its unique artistic character, impressive *Capoeira* shows (an Afro-Brazilian martial art integrating elements of dance, acrobatics, and music), and beautiful trails leading to lovely nearby beaches with stunning views along the way made it truly memorable.

I made many wonderful friends in Rio de Janeiro, one of them being an outstanding Capoeira artist, Benedito, whom I met at Casa Rosa in the Laranjeiras neighborhood. Casa Rosa was one of my favorite hangouts on Sunday afternoons, where people would gather for a *feijoada*, the traditional black bean stew served with a variety of sides, enjoy a *roda de samba*, a Samba band with everyone dancing to their beats, and watch mesmerizing *Capoeira* performances.

I also loved taking long walks in the Floresta da Tijuca. In Rio, you have the luxury of literally walking from the city right into the tropical rainforest, with its amazing waterfalls and mysterious ponds. Sometimes, I would go hiking deeper into the wilderness with a friend from dance who knew his way around. And then, in 2010,…

…I finally went paragliding. Every time I'd take the bus or van down to Barra da Tijuca beach, I'd look up at Pedra da Gávea in São Conrado and think: One day, I'm gonna do this! And now, that moment had come. My friends Sabrina and Giselle called me one day and asked if I wanted to join them. Did I want to go? Of course, I did! I was thrilled!

Giselle had a friend who worked there, and he was the one who tandem jumped with me. Before we took off, he mentioned that a woman had died a few weeks earlier because she hadn't been properly secured. Apparently, her harness was unclipped during a wait due to some minor weather condition, and they forgot to secure her before the jump. As soon as they ran into the air, she fell and died. After hearing this, I double-checked my harness very carefully. I must admit, I was a bit nervous. While I'm very adventurous in other ways, extreme sports or jumping into the void weren't among the activities I'd usually do without a second thought.

But there was no doubt I wanted to do this. From my rappelling experience back in Petrópolis, I knew that the most exhilarating and memorable adventures are those that require that first leap into the unknown. And so, I experienced one of the most breathtaking views over the lush, rainforest-covered hills and the pristine beaches south of Rio de Janeiro, stretching out over the ocean. The one thing I was still a bit anxious about was the landing. However, knowing we would either land on a small area with soft grass or on beach sand calmed me. While my landing wasn't the most perfect of all time, it was good enough. No one was hurt, and a slightly imperfect touchdown couldn't diminish the rest of the experience.

Rio de Janeiro is truly a marvelous place! When people ask me which of the places I've lived in is my favorite, I am often tempted to say Rio because of its incredible natural beauty: the hills, beaches, waterfalls, and tropical vegetation are all part of the city and its immediate surroundings. However, my original home near the Bavarian Alps deserves a five-star rating as well, though I probably took it for granted when I was young. Then I think of Madrid, Munich, Buenos Aires, and New York City with their beautiful architecture and unique flair. Answering the question becomes impossible... but Rio always tops the list.

I have countless stories from my time in Rio, like raking in the Carnival madness and partying wildly with Luciana, Sabrina, and Cris; the night I ran for my life after watching a theater performance in downtown Rio, or the time I ran from burglars with my friend Carole from Belgium. Sadly, they caught her bag while I escaped, running faster, but thankfully, nothing more serious happened… not this time nor the other times I'd put myself into risky situations. I somehow always was protected in this sense.

As I was having what would be my last meal of *carne seca com aipim* (typical Brazilian dried meat with cassava) while sipping a *caipirinha de maracujá* (passion fruit caipirinha) with my friend Ahmyna, I was thinking to myself: Isn't it astounding how resilient humans are? If I had known before what I was going to go through, would I ever have chosen to move to Rio? – Certainly not. However, if I'd known what was going to happen, then I'd also have done everything differently, haha. The morale of the story being: In hindsight, everything seems so obvious, but while we're in the midst of it, it doesn't. So, all the "should'ves" and "would'ves" really make no sense at all. We are exactly where we are supposed to be to learn our lessons, whether they are pleasant or painful.

I was up for a new start, and that's all that counted… even though the Rio chapter would still follow me a little while.

Leadership Wisdom – Key Takeaways

Moving Forward Requires a Self-Empowering Mindset

As painful as the story with my fraudulent business partner was, it taught me a significant lesson and spurred considerable growth in my life mastery. It forced me to step out of victimhood and into a self-empowering mindset. Operating in victim mode keeps us stuck, making it difficult to move forward despite our efforts. Pushing our way upstream just doesn't work very well.

It was time for me to take my share of responsibility in the story: I hadn't done my due diligence on the guy. As it later turned out, he'd committed some other crooked things with other people who'd trusted him. I was unaware of this… Maybe I should have asked around more, although I may not have found out what I know now either by doing that. Most importantly, though, I could have listened more closely to my intuition. Because at some point along the way, there was a voice that whispered: "Be careful." It wasn't loud enough, or I refused to listen because this collaboration seemed so enticing, and finally, I wouldn't have to do everything by myself but rather with someone local who "knew his way around."

Simultaneously, I didn't want to fall into the trap of taking all the responsibility because I was already beating myself up too much, and forgiving oneself is often the hardest thing to do. Assuming the entire responsibility, although the other person clearly did something wrong, is yet another symptom of being in victim mode; it's like self-flagellation and suffering from it at the same time.

I had to find my way out of victimhood and into a self-empowering mindset. This shift allowed me to take control of my life and decisions, learning from the past while not being defined by it.

What are you still clinging to that you need to let go of so you can move forward with your vision and your plans for the life you want and for the leader you want to be? What's missing for you to feel truly self-empowered? Because remember this: No one can empower you but yourself. Your power is already inside of you. You just need to connect with it and to practice feeling it. That's all.

In fact, there is no real outside power. Your intrinsic power is the one thing you can always rely on, and no one can ever take it away from you unless you give it up to them.

Self-Forgiveness Is Critical for Advancement

Judging and resenting ourselves leads to feelings of guilt, one of the lowest-vibration emotions on the scale. Guilt, like any other so-called "negative" emotion, serves a temporary purpose. It signals us to avoid repeating certain behaviors in order to improve. However, prolonged guilt is detrimental to our self-esteem, self-confidence, and self-belief. It prevents us from moving beyond the past and embracing new opportunities. Without forgiveness – especially self-forgiveness – we remain anchored in the past, reinforcing negative belief patterns that limit what we can achieve and bar us from digging deeper into our potential.

Forgiveness is an expression of love. And if that is so, then self-forgiveness is an expression of self-love. For me, forgiving the person who wronged me was far easier than forgiving myself. You might relate to this: Are you your own harshest critic? Do you find it hard to practice self-compassion… self-love? Do you hold yourself to higher standards than you do others? It's common to justify this by claiming, "I just have high standards." High standards are commendable, but judging yourself for not knowing better in the past won't help you improve in the future. In hindsight, everything appears more obvious than it does in the moment. You couldn't have known better at the time; you know better now. This understanding is why you endured the pain in the first place. Learning through pain is a part of life. What truly matters is the lesson, recognizing any patterns that need breaking to avoid repeating the same mistakes.

What patterns have you identified in your life that you've either resolved or still need to address? What patterns in your team need attention to prevent future conflicts or failures?

Standing up for What's Right Makes You Feel Good

I sure have had many opportunities in my life where I could have gone for the comfortable choice, but I opted for what has felt right to me, even when it was uncomfortable because it required doing research, informing myself from not-so-readily-available sources, and swimming against the mainstream. It's what respectable leaders do: They consult many different and diverse sources to make sure they are well-informed, they question orders, and they stand up for what's right, even if their stance is not the popular one or if they risk the position.

As a leader, how can you broaden your understanding of both your work environment and the world at large? How can you stay optimally informed? And how can you leverage this knowledge to serve, protect and support those you lead? It's one of those things worth journaling on.

And you know what? It feels so tremendously good to do the right thing. This feeling alone is sufficient reward.

Walking the Line Between the Flow of Life and Deliberated Choices Is an Art

You never know what else life could have in store for you if you don't sometimes let loose and follow your inner guidance. We are so conditioned to do what we "should do" and want what we "should want" that we don't even realize that we may not be on the ideal track for the life we want to live; we don't even recognize what it is that we *really* want, deep down.

So, next time you spot an opportunity on the horizon, put your fear aside and dare to explore it. I'm not saying you should grab just any proposal or job offer. You still want to figure out first whether it's aligned with what you really want. For example, I did not take a job offer for Asia once, which was very tempting as I would have been traveling between four Asian countries, but it wasn't the right fit for me at the time… and probably never would have been. There was also an option of a temporary job in the Mumbai office; and while I'd always wanted to travel to India, this particular opportunity was just not was I was looking for at the time. Instead, the consulting contract with DeRemate in Argentina popped up in my email… and that one *did* feel right.

When fate presents you with a chance, you always have a choice: Take it or not take it. What matters is that you make a conscious, empowered decision, rather than shying away from it because of fear or self-doubt.

And when life throws you a curveball, recognize the opportunity in it. Any circumstance, whether we perceive it as good or bad, as pleasant or painful, as exhilarating or terrifying, bears a chance for us to learn and grow. Whenever you experience a setback, ask yourself: "What's the lesson here? Is there a pattern? What can I learn so I can avoid a similar situation in the past?" Then detach yourself emotionally so you can move on and create a better future for yourself.

Resilience in the Face of Setbacks Is a Catalyst for Growth

My experience with a fraudulent business partner in Rio de Janeiro was a harsh reminder that setbacks are inevitable as we move through life. What matters most is how we respond to them. Instead of being defeated by betrayal, I (eventually, not immediately) chose to view it as a learning opportunity, a chance to strengthen my resolve and sharpen my instincts. Resilience isn't just about bouncing back; it's about using challenges as steppingstones for personal and professional growth. When we face setbacks with determination and an open mind, they become catalysts that propel us toward greater wisdom and success.

Ever faced a setback? I bet you have – who hasn't? Here's a quick exercise: Grab a piece of paper and draw three columns. At the top of each, write down one of your biggest setbacks. Now, under each one, list the lessons you learned and how those experiences have contributed to your growth. You might be surprised at how much you've gained from those challenges.

This is how you turn a setback into a gain, or a loss into a win.

*

When I boarded the plane to New York, I hadn't planned to leave permanently. I simply wasn't prepared to part with Samba de Gafieira dancing, the tropical climate, my favorite landscapes, and – once again – my friends. My intention was to divide my time between Rio de Janeiro and New York City. Whether that plan came to fruition, I'll reveal in the upcoming chapters.

Chapter 10

Taking a Bite of the Big Apple – New York, New York!

Lessons in Flexibility and Mobility

My arrival in New York was nothing short of exciting. Despite having visited the city a couple of times before, there was still so much to discover! I loved New York's architecture, from the charming townhouses to the historic buildings. Plus, it was a relief not to have to watch out for my security as much as in Rio, although I had gotten used to that and it had become second nature. New York certainly has its dicey areas at night, but security only became a significant concern during the 2020 lockdown. Areas like the Port Authority bus station felt eerie during that time, with only drug addicts and homeless people lingering, a stark contrast to the bustling atmosphere before and after. But I'm jumping ahead...

I initially found temporary housing and moved around Manhattan, staying in various neighborhoods for a month or two... in Chelsea, Midtown, Two Bridges, Gramercy Park, Williamsburg, Upper West, and even up in Inwood. Eventually, I settled into a longer-term apartment, occupying a floor in a townhouse on the lovely tree-lined West 130th Steet in Central Harlem. Later, I moved a few blocks down to West Harlem, right on the corner of Central Park, on West 110th Street. Harlem quickly became my favorite neighborhood with its many restaurants, music joints like Silvana and Shrine, and African stores. My preferred areas were 116th St. as well as Lenox, just above and below 125th. There was always something happening there, and Central Park was right next door, too!

Speaking of Central Park, one of the things I loved most about NYC was the free summer concerts in the parks. From Central Park to Prospect Park in Brooklyn, there was always something happening every week during July and August. Amazing bands from all over the world played in both big and small parks across the boroughs, making the city feel like a continuous, joyful festival.

Of course, dancing remained a vital part of my life. In the absence of my favorite Brazilian dances, I turned to Salsa and Bachata for social dancing. Tuesday nights were reserved for Salsa at Taj, while Saturday nights were dedicated to mixed Latin dancing at Club Cache. Later, I added Thursday nights at Gonzalez y Gonzalez in SOHO, and occasionally ventured to Bembe in Brooklyn or down to Favela Cubana in NOHO for Cuban Salsa, as opposed to the more prevalent "Salsa on 2" in NYC.

Dancing is how I met my first big love in New York City, Miguel. It's true that dancing releases oxytocin, the "bonding hormone" or "love hormone," which is known for its healing effect. In partner dancing, the effect is doubled: both from the dancing and the embrace, and it sure did its magic beyond healing in this case. Though our initial relationship felt somewhat one-sided, we reconnected a few years later when Miguel unexpectedly reached out to invite me to a lavish dinner at my favorite restaurant at the time, the fancifully decorated Spice Market in the Meatpacking District (which, unfortunately, has since closed).

A few months after my arrival in the Big Apple, I added Angolan dances like Kizomba and Semba, as well as Haitian Kompa. Compared to Tango and Samba de Gafieira, these were relatively easy dances that I picked up on the dance floor, aside from a couple of initial Kizomba/Semba workshops. Dancing at my all-time favorite spot for these dances, Favela Cubana, is also how I met my best friend for the years to come, Chris. Thanks to Chris, I experienced some of the most exhilarating moments dancing Kompa, including live concerts at SOBs and traditional Haitian bands that visited at certain times of the year, mostly playing at events in Long Island. I was often the only non-Haitian person in the room, but I was used to this scenario from my travels and other moments, and I found this rather interesting – observing the dynamics of people reacting to me, comments in the ladies' room, like "you and your husband, you dance so beautifully together." (Ha, no problem, let them think we're married… I love this guy anyway!). I'd take the Long Island Railroad to those venues and return to the city in the early morning hours – often enough, Chris and I would be waiting in his car for the first train back to Manhattan. Finally at home, feet burning from hours of dancing in high heels, I'd fall into bed exhausted but happy.

Dancing with Chris all night felt like heaven on Earth. Not just because of the dancing itself but also because of the special connection we shared. Spending time with him always felt like a blessing. Sweet memories indeed.

During my early years in New York City, while still traveling back and forth to Rio de Janeiro, I wrote several articles for the German *dance for you* magazine in English. The first article was about a Brazilian couple, Janete and Leandro da Silva, who danced and choreographed together. Later, I occasionally took some Samba classes with Janete. Back in Brazil, I interviewed dancers from Sonia Destri's Companhia Urbana de Dança and two of my Gafieira instructors to write more articles for the magazine. I also wrote about an immensely talented young dancer and client from Macau – dear to my heart.

I had an Equinox gym membership, which allowed me access to fitness, yoga, and dance classes (and the sauna, which was a blessing during the cold NYC winters) at all their gyms across the city. Later, I switched to dance classes at various studios, taking House Dance with Kim Holmes, Afro Urban with Angel Kaba, Kukuwa with Cassandra Nuamah, and West African with Vado Diomande and occasionally Maguette Camara. And eventually, I discovered my passion for Congolese Ndombolo with Nkumu Katalay. Why mention the names of these amazing dance teachers? Most importantly, they deserve the spotlight and recognition. Additionally, for the dance aficionados among you, these names might be familiar, or you might live in the places described in this book and want to take classes yourself. Well, you've just met some of the best!

But enough about dance… for now (more about it later)! Let's shift our focus to more serious matters because, truth be told, my first few years in New York City were a mixed bag of experiences.

Even at a distance, I still was dealing with those frustrating civil servants to close my business in Brazil, something I had paid my accountant to do twice, even from a distance. Would it surprise you to hear that, to this day, I am not certain my business was ever properly closed, despite completing all the paperwork and paying the fees twice? There's a local saying: "It's harder to close a business than it is to open one in Rio." I've been told that, in order to avoid the hassle, many people use a *favela* (slum) as the official location of their business. However, I hadn't done that, and so I had to contend with the usual paperwork ordeal, but that was just one part of the "Rio mess" I was still untangling…

As mentioned earlier, I held an investor's visa with the intention of renewing it to transition to a new business while maintaining my residency permit. Initially, my plan involved splitting my time between Rio and New York, although the reality unfolded quite differently. However, I did split my time – and energy! – between the two places while still resolving everything… that much is true. More details on this in the next chapter.

Leadership Wisdom – Key Takeaways

Sometimes, We Gotta Make a Move

Throughout my life, there have been moments when I moved because I wanted to or because an opportunity arose. At other times, I was nudged to change locations, such as my move from Rio to New York, which wasn't entirely voluntary. This doesn't mean it wasn't a choice. We always have choices, even when they seem hidden. Moving is one of those decisions.

I've moved countless times: to new neighborhoods, cities, countries, and even continents. People often ask if I'm running away from something. I assure you, I'm not. Moving across continents and immersing myself in new cultures and languages alone is no easy feat. It's not about convenience or escape. Anyone who has moved intercontinentally knows that it's all but convenient. Each move contributes to my growth. It feels like the Universe nudges me onward when I've learned all I can from a place. If I resist, circumstances arise that push me to move.

If you find your life unsatisfactory, take action to change it. Don't operate on autopilot. You are meant to create your life by design, not to remain stuck.

- Are you bored? Seek a new adventure or challenge.
- Are you in an environment that no longer suits you? Change it or find a new one.
- Are you in a toxic relationship, at work or at home? Get out of it.

Sometimes, you gotta make a move – literally! If your current location feels wrong, consider relocating. Not every place on Earth is right for you. It's up to you to discover which ones are.

You might consult location astrology, but if that's not your thing, rely on your intuition. Connect with your heart and ask: What do I really want? What do I need and where can I get it?

Remember, you can always move again. Nothing is forever, and newness can catapult you like a fresh breeze towards *freakin' amazing.*

*

During my frequent flights between Rio and New York, a whirlwind of thoughts and emotions consumed me. It was an emotionally demanding period. I still grappled with regret, self-resentment, and guilt. I missed many aspects of Rio and mourned personal losses while also embracing new experiences. I left friends behind in Rio and forged new bonds in NYC. As someone naturally attuned to emotions, managing them has often been a challenge. In the past, I didn't realize this and struggled to control the drama that sneaked into my life. Over time, I learned to harness the positive aspects of my emotional nature, using my feelings as guides rather than letting them control me. But let's move forward in my story!

Chapter 11

Cleaning up the Mess – While Keeping Spirits High

Lessons in Patience, Letting Go, Taking a Leap, and Leading with Passion

Like anywhere else in the world, immigration systems can be (many are!) corrupt, varying only in the methods of their corruption. The Immigration Police in Rio de Janeiro, located at the Galeão International Airport, were no exception. I had amassed a stack of paperwork as thick as the Yellow Pages of a metropolis (for the younger generation reading this: the old phone books), with every single copy and signature meticulously certified (as is required in Brazil), and a significant amount of money went into this documentation. I even hired an accountant to help me compile everything.

Despite my efforts, they began "losing" papers over time, claiming I hadn't submitted them. I knew I had, as I kept copies of everything. It became clear that the officials were intentionally suppressing documents to pressure me into paying bribes. One morning, I had an appointment at 8am with an officer who didn't show up until 11:30am. Another time, I waited all day only to be told they were closing, forcing me to return the next day.

I loved Rio and wanted to spend part of the year there even after moving to NYC. That's why I kept my belongings in storage and frequently flew back to Rio to deal with the Immigration Police and follow up on my paperwork. However, because I refused to pay bribes, I ultimately lost my residency permit, despite all the effort, time, and money I invested, including travel costs from New York. I know for sure that the officer wanted a bribe because he gave me his personal cell phone number. I never called him, but it was a clear sign of his intentions.

Meanwhile, I was juggling three lawsuits against the dance academy owner, each with a different lawyer because no single attorney wanted to handle all three cases. One lawsuit was for the money he embezzled, another for the payment I made to use his brand for the dance portion of my business, and the third for the prepaid dance classes I never attended after discovering his fraudulent behavior.

When two of them finally came through, the money I got from them in reais was worth a third, and I also had to pay my lawyers a percentage, so there was little left. I was still grateful for it, also because I had stood up for myself, rather than just being walked over.

At some point, I felt compelled to return to Rio de Janeiro and sell my belongings that had been in storage since I first left the city. Arriving on the last day of December, I was just in time to join the euphoric New Year's celebration at Copacabana Beach, with its three music stages and infectious partying. It was the perfect uplift before facing the trials and tribulations ahead.

Despite having hoped the storage facility would assist in selling some of my furniture remotely over time, they didn't cooperate, leaving me to quickly figure out how to sell everything and donate what remained during my brief visit. Thankfully, my friend Sabrina graciously opened her home to me and allowed me to store some last items until they sold, including my favorite-ever bamboo bed from Bali, which had moved with me many times – from Munich to San Francisco to Buenos Aires to Rio de Janeiro. Meanwhile, my loyal friend Chris from New York sent encouraging messages daily. I am deeply grateful to both of them.

I paid for storage and insurance all those months – for nothing! If I had known sooner that my visa wouldn't be renewed, I would've sold everything at a better price. Instead, I had just one day to organize the sale. The storage owners reluctantly gave me this day to clear out my belongings. I hustled to promote my items online and reached out to friends who might want pots, furniture, books, or any of the other things I'd collected over time.

With the clock ticking, I managed to sell almost everything in one day at the storage unit. Raquel, a friend, helped out with the sale. In exchange, she took some boxes and my large, beloved couch for a small sum. I had done a lot of pre-work, trying to sell things online and inviting people to the "garage sale." But one day wasn't enough time to go through it all. I expected more people to show up, but fortunately, some did, at least. For the remaining items, I hired a truck the next day to transport it to my friend's house and resolve the rest from there.

I was glad to see my djembe and other musical instruments go to a friend from capoeira, my best kitchen items to Rodrigo, who was setting up a new place, and most of the towels and sheets to a guy starting a bed & breakfast. A young couple took my favorite kitchen furniture, including an exclusive designer piece, for their first home together, and Olaf, a friendly Russian guy, bought my beloved Balinese bamboo bed.

In just one day, I managed to sell almost everything in storage, except for the books I couldn't take and some major items I gifted to the storage workers. Later, I realized many things were missing: a silver vase, a silver picture frame, tools, and gifts from family and friends. They had a list of contents for insurance, so they knew what should have been there. They had also mixed my items with other people's belongings, as there was no dedicated unit for me. This storage was a mess! Should you ever need to store your things in Rio, call me up and I'll tell you where *not* to do it. (Just to be clear, I'd never seen the facility itself before my return, as they'd picked up my belongings at my home.)

I salvaged as many books as possible to donate to a bookstore that only accepted Portuguese books. I sold a few books in other languages online and gifted others to friends, but I still had many left, including valuable dictionaries, coffee-table books, gifts that held sentimental value, and books with content that was of major personal significance for me. It was a significant moment of letting go – those books, the bamboo bed, and the gifts that meant so much to me emotionally.

Despite paying monthly premiums, the insurance never paid a dime. I suspect the storage company may have pocketed that money instead of paying it to the insurance. They gave me too many reasons to believe this.

But let's turn to happier times: After spending the entire day at the storage facility without more than a banana and water to sustain us, Raquel and I were utterly exhausted and famished when we finally took the subway back to Botafogo that night. Throughout the day, I had been too preoccupied to even consider food... Until we decided to treat ourselves to fried fish and beers on Leme beach. It was a feast! When I finally got home that night, I collapsed into bed, physically and emotionally exhausted, and slept like a log.

The very next day, I embarked on an exciting trip to Ilha de Paquetá, a charming island off the coast of Rio where there are no cars, and many visitors rent bikes to explore. I had visited before with my friend Marianne, but this time was different: I went with a group of young boys. But let me back up a bit.

During one of my trips back to Rio, while I was sorting through my many to-dos and cleaning up the mess caused by the business partner debacle, I met Edie, an American filmmaker, at the bank who needed assistance. I helped her resolve her issue, and in turn, she told me about a home for about 20 young boys aged 6 to 14. These boys had been removed from their homes due to domestic violence or drug abuse. Hearing that they craved attention, given there were only two educators for the entire group, I decided to take the long bus ride to their neighborhood to meet them.

To describe the place as "lively" would be an understatement. It happened to be haircut day, so some boys were proudly showing off their new hairstyles, while others were still waiting their turn with the hairdresser who had set up his salon in the yard. Each boy had a key to a small drawer or compartment where they locked their modest personal belongings. Aside from the clothes on their backs and flip-flops on their feet, they typically owned a couple more t-shirts, shorts, and one or two small items. One boy, particularly talented in making little figures and keychains from beads, touched me deeply when he gifted me one of his creations.

On this trip to Rio, I decided to collect some money to bring the boys gifts: a brand-new t-shirt and a pair of flip-flops for each, along with exotic snacks from abroad, which they devoured. Upon arriving at the house, I was greeted with hugs and screams of joy, which were almost overwhelming and brought tears to my eyes. The educators allowed me to hand out the t-shirts myself but kept the flip-flops for when they'd need new ones.

During that visit, I invited the boys to participate in a visioning game. We were seated on the floor and a bench in a community room, and I thought to myself, everyone deserves the chance to dream. So, I asked them to close their eyes and envision themselves flying on an airplane to any destination they desired – be it a distant country, a local spot, a place they'd seen on TV, or an entirely imaginary location. Together, we traveled in our minds, each of us directing their own mind movie, crafting mini-visions. Afterwards, we talked about the significance of first creating what you want in your mind. The kids thoroughly enjoyed the game – after all, what child doesn't love to daydream?

The educators invited me to accompany the boys on a trip to Ilha de Paquetá the day after my storage "garage sale." I was excited about seeing them again. However, the morning after the move, I woke up exhausted to the sound of my alarm clock. My body felt like a wet bag of potatoes from moving boxes and furniture as well as unpacking and repacking countless items the day before. I debated whether I really wanted to get up and head over to the pier. Eventually, at the last minute, I decided yes! I rushed out to catch the bus, but since it was a Saturday, the buses were on a slower schedule. I was on the lookout for taxis, but none came by. I thought I'd definitely miss the ferry boat they'd be on, and I regretted getting up so late, when usually, I like to be early for critical situations like this.

But eventually, a bus showed up, and miraculously, I made it to the ferry station on time! I was running with literally a couple of minutes left before the boat would leave. Imagine my joy when I saw some of the boys still standing at the ticket booth while their educators distributed tickets. When they saw me, three of them came running over, one snatched my bag to carry it for me, so we'd be faster, and we all ran to the ferry amidst big smiles and loud laughter. No amount of money could pay for the happy faces and warm hugs that welcomed me. It's indescribable. It felt like we deeply appreciated each other's company. We sat on the floor of the overbooked ferry, the boys leaning on me and telling jokes, all of us grateful that I'd made it.

On the island, we rented bikes for everyone and a tandem for one of the educators to ride with a little boy who had a leg disability and impaired eyesight. He was also the funniest and cheekiest of the group. In contrast, another boy was very closed off. I guess he had already experienced a lot of hardship in his young life to be so angry and sad. He didn't want to mingle much, despite the others having the time of their lives biking through the island, eating ice cream, and enjoying a very special experience.

After an exhilarating day on the island, we returned the bikes and boarded the ferry back to the city. On the way back, the boys were much quieter, worn out from their adventures. Some even drifted off into a contented sleep. At the pier, it was time to say goodbye. This was the last time I saw them. As I write this, a trip back to Brazil is long overdue. I often wonder what has become of those boys. I hope many have found their way back to safer homes by now.

Leadership Wisdom – Key Takeaways

Letting Go of the Old Makes Space for the New

The night I left the storage facility after selling most of my things, a huge wave of relief washed over me. Yet, it also marked the start of an intense detachment process, especially for some of my favorite items, like gifts from family and friends and my beloved books. This process lingered for years.

I couldn't possibly move everything, and it seemed impractical to incur the cost of moving only part of it, especially since I'd opted for a furnished apartment in New York for the time being. I wanted to stay flexible, as I was toying with the idea of potentially moving to Africa. While this hasn't happened (yet), not having so much "stuff" gave me a sense of liberty. I felt more mobile again, and maybe that's what I needed then, even if I ended up staying in New York longer than in many other places before, with numerous trips to Africa and elsewhere. (More about that later.)

In the end, this detachment made me more resilient. Giving things away freed up stuck energy, allowing it to flow more freely. By letting go, I created room for the new.

The same happens when we let go of old beliefs, grudges, or resentments. These stuck emotions and related thoughts can occupy too much valuable real estate in our minds. Once we free ourselves from these self-imposed shackles, we can breathe and move more freely.

You've probably heard that 90% of our thoughts on any given day are similar to the day before. What if we could make the majority of these 90% thoughts that actually serve us? What if we could let go of disempowering thoughts and replace them with empowering ones? This takes daily practice, but it's worth it. Try it! It will ripple off to your team. You could even make it a team exercise! Be creative when teaching your team a mindset that supports not just their work but also their overall well-being. Inspire them to reflect on these topics, and you might see miracles.

The Greatest Successes Come When We Dare to Jump

Sometimes, the most memorable experiences are just a leap away. This principle isn't limited to extreme sports like paragliding, bungee jumping, or skydiving. In your career, your most desired goals might be unlocked by that crucial first step. A baby step can often set things in motion, but there are moments when courage demands a larger leap or even If you wait for everything to align perfectly before taking action, you may wait indefinitely – because that ideal moment might never materialize. And you'll never feel completely prepared. Sometimes, trusting that you're ready enough is the only preparation you need.

Perfectionism can be paralyzing. Could it be preventing you from taking that leap forward in your career right now? The only true failure is failing to try... failing to seize the chance to pursue what you want most.

If you aspire to a leadership role, start by leading yourself! And if an opportunity nods enticingly, take the plunge! You might land more softly than you expect. And if the landing is a bit rough, you've still gained valuable experience for next time.

When We Give or Lead with Compassion, the Rewards Are Immediate

Spending time with those kids wasn't just meaningful for *them*; it was profoundly fulfilling and precious to *me*. Witnessing their genuine smiles brought instant gratification. It's amazing how deeply satisfying it is to receive unfiltered appreciation.

Leading your team with compassion and attentiveness yields similar rewards. As social beings, we thrive on connection, sharing, and mutual support. Anything contrary goes against our natural instincts. Some team members may lack social connections due to relocation, distance from family, or personal losses. While I'm not keen on the notion of a workplace as a "big family," I believe in fostering healthy relationships among colleagues and managers. This not only enhances work quality but also minimizes unnecessary conflicts and friction, which favors productivity.

Encourage your team to excel by prioritizing compassionate leadership: Actively engage with your team members. Start today, and lead with compassion to transform your team's dynamic and performance as a direct result of your compassionate approach. Here are a few options you can implement right away:

- Schedule a one-on-one meeting with each team member this week to discuss their current challenges and needs. Show genuine interest in their well-being and offer support where possible. Witness the immediate impact – you may be in for a surprise! Observe the positive changes in their engagement because of you showing that you care. You may also want to implement regular check-ins, where you personally connect with each team member, for instance every two weeks or once a month.

- Create a support network by setting up a peer mentorship program, where team members can offer and receive guidance, fostering a collaborative environment.
- Recognize and celebrate wins: Regularly acknowledge and celebrate the efforts and successes of your team, reinforcing a culture of appreciation.

The Biggest Cost Is Not Always About Money

While the immediate loss of money was steep, the biggest cost of my business partner experience wasn't financial. It was two-fold:

Firstly, the cost of "cleaning up the mess." The time and energy investment this required significantly slowed down my new business venture in New York. My energy was split between two locations, with the old one being a source of immense stress. This constant back-and-forth between New York and Rio de Janeiro caused significant delays, deviating far from my original plan of smoothly dividing my time between the two cities.

Secondly, I lost my self-esteem and confidence, which I had to rebuild from scratch – from "below zero." This was a major setback for me, especially since I'd spent years working on my confidence, which used to be a long-term challenge in my life.

But here's the thing: This experience taught me how to rebuild confidence from the ground up, addressing the root causes of our insecurities and applying techniques that proved successful. Later, I could share this knowledge and wisdom with my clients who also struggled with confidence, and I even collected many of them in my book *Speak up, Stand out and Shine – Speak Powerfully in Any Situation*, where I share tips and tools to prepare for speaking situations.

Nothing is a waste of time when used as an opportunity for growth. Some of the toughest challenges can become our biggest opportunities, but we must recognize them as such. Staying in victim mode prevents this transformation.

Reflect on a recent painful experience. How can you turn it into an opportunity for personal growth? And how can you do the same for your team, starting now and moving forward?

*

After returning from Rio, I woke up to a Harlem yard buried in knee-high snow. The shift from Rio de Janeiro's tropical summer to New York's biting winter was jarring. Though I had made significant progress, the Rio chapter remained unfinished. For now, though, I eagerly anticipated dancing Thursday nights away at Favela Cubana with Chris, and I had plans for some intense networking.

Chapter 12
Empire State of Mind: Shapeshifting in New York

Lessons in Rebuilding Confidence and Networking

After moving to New York City, without a local network and little idea about starting a business (other than a B&B or a dance & wellness studio, which was not in my plans in this new location), I was trying to figure out what to do next. I needed to "re-invent myself," as we sometimes say, although it's really about how to move into the next bigger version of ourselves, isn't it? The question on my mind was: How could I weave together all my eclectic experiences into a meaningful new chapter that I'd feel passionate about? My multinational and multilingual background, the various roles I'd had in the professional services industry, in corporate, at a start-up, my translation work, my holistic and mindset studies, my passion for travel and dance, and, of course, my personal experiences and all the lessons I had learned over the years – how would it all fit together?

The first idea that came to mind was to work with performing artists, especially dancers, due to my love for dance. For a while, I did just that, with some of my first clients being a young professional dancer in Macau and a coach/choreographer for a group of dancers in New York. I also organized a few meetups and smaller events at my home, where we focused on money mindset and related topics. My initial company was even registered as Transform Your Dance Performance. However, I quickly discovered that many performing artists suffered from the "starving artist" syndrome, making it challenging to encourage them to invest in themselves, even though my rates were more than affordable.

I began networking outside of the dance scene, and I clearly remember how difficult it was at first. I was still in the process of regaining my confidence *poco a poco* and transitioning back into the English-speaking zone after seven years of primarily speaking Spanish and Portuguese. I recall one particular entrepreneurial networking event where I was testing out my early attempts at an elevator pitch, which, admittedly, were not great. One lady responded to me, quite rudely, "What does that even mean?" I will never forget that moment. I left the event earlier than planned, emotionally drained and crying. To clarify, I mostly cried out of anger, which is my "go-to" emotion when I'm not at my best. When something like this happens, I default to anger. I have learned that about myself over the years, and I've also worked on managing this.

In any case, I wasn't one to give up easily. Over time, I discovered smaller, friendlier networking circles. Still, it wasn't always easy to approach people and start a conversation. While I had made new friends and acquaintances in each place I moved to, I had never really needed to network professionally or outside of dance.

Networking requires practice, unless you're a "networking natural," which I was not. Remarkably, over time, I gained a reputation as a connector. I even scored free tickets to otherwise paid events because I brought so much positive energy. Someone once told me, "You always light up the room at my events. Want to help me greet people and get free tickets in return?" Of course, I wanted that! It gave me an excellent excuse to talk to everyone, at least briefly.

In a short period, I built a vast network. After each event, I'd connect with everyone I met on LinkedIn. My LinkedIn network grew organically from zero to almost 30,000 connections in just a few years. Later, a LinkedIn expert urged me to reduce that number drastically to about 8,000. Whether that was a good move or not, I don't know – likely not. But after strong and long resistance, I let myself be persuaded… just to notice later that I'd lost a lot of precious contacts in the process. Again: Always follow your intuition over other people's recommendations. When it doesn't feel right, don't do it!

In any case, my network grew exponentially – both online and offline – and even internationally. Over time, I added critical contacts in several African countries, which later allowed me to travel for projects. But I'm getting ahead of myself…

While building my business, I enrolled in a group program offered by a well-known coach. I absorbed an overwhelming amount of business knowledge, much of which I hadn't even realized I needed. The program also provided valuable networking opportunities. It felt like a huge investment at the time, but it turned out to be one of the better decisions compared to other programs I later invested in. Some of those were repetitive, overloaded with material, too cookie-cutter, and lacked personalized coaching.

I won't name names, but it's important to remember that not all coaching programs are created equal. One program I joined was so basic and ideologically driven that I requested to withdraw and rescind my agreement. Like any industry, the coaching world has its share of black sheep. Some big-name coaches are better salespeople (or they *have* better salespeople) than they are coaches. My advice for anyone seeking a coach is to have a direct conversation with the coach before committing, or in the case of a large group program, to thoroughly vet the coach to ensure a good fit. What works for your friend or colleague might not work for you. Coaching, even in a group setting, is a deeply personal experience. And when it's the right match, it can change your life for the better – big time!

Through my networking activities, it soon became apparent that I'd have more success working with professionals outside of the arts. This realization led me to rebrand my business as Transform Your Performance. The concept of "performance" applies universally, and I still liked the resonance of the name.

I soon began hosting my own events. For my first half-day session in Midtown, I had five participants. At the next event, I doubled that number to ten. By my third event, after making over

200 phone calls (many during long walks in Central Park), I had over 40 attendees.

Initially, my events attracted mostly women, though I later hosted several with mixed crowds. Gradually, I discovered that my ideal clients were employed leaders or business owners with teams, primarily women at the time. However, over the years, I have also worked very successfully with quite a few men.

Before long, I found myself speaking at prestigious organizations like AMA and PMI. I reached out to New York City's numerous banks and law firms, securing invitations to speak at financial giants such as BNY Mellon, BNP Paribas, Barclays, Northern Trust, and Lloyds, as well as prominent firms like Kirkland, Duval & Stachenfeld, and Chapman and Cutler. My speaking engagements expanded to other states, including law schools, various summits, and conferences. I was also invited to coach at a major women's conference at the Gaylord Resort & Convention Center National Harbor, Maryland, for five consecutive years. While not all events were paid, they were usually effective for lead generation, and I've gained many clients from these audiences, and I also got to teach top-rated online group coaching sessions for the organizer's audience.

One particularly enjoyable highlight was when I was serving as the keynote speaker and panel moderator for three esteemed interior designers at an event hosted by the Interior Design Society (IDS) of New York, led by my business friend Julie Schuster. Following that, I inspired an audience gathered by The Professional Association for Interior Designers (ASID).

My journey also took me back to BCG as an external trainer in California and South Africa, and I was featured in an Alumni highlight interview by BCG New York.

I joined the Leadership Team of the Financial Women's Association New York (FWA), co-chairing two committees, organizing events with successful women in Finance, and speaking at a couple of FWA events myself. Throughout this period, I networked relentlessly across New York City and participated in nationwide conferences hosted by renowned coaches.

As you can see, my schedule was packed with activity. Not every endeavor proved successful or beneficial for my business, but each one was a valuable lesson in its own way. My network grew exponentially, both online and offline, reaching new heights and expanding globally. I had set an unstoppable network into motion.

Leadership Wisdom – Key Takeaways

Regain Confidence as You Regrow Hair

My confidence was literally below level zero when I moved to New York to launch a new chapter of my life. Not the greatest way to start. But deep down, I knew I could do it!

Setbacks can make you feel like you've lost your self-esteem and confidence, but it doesn't have to last long. It's only temporary. Just as hair grows back with care, so does confidence. The sooner you address it, the easier it becomes to overcome. So, snap out of it! Move on and create your next big thing!

I know, that's sometimes easier said than done… If you feel like you could do with help around raising your confidence and self-belief, find an expert to guide you. It's also one of my specialties! Just reach out and let's have a conversation about how I can assist you so you can accelerate the process and feel better faster.

Don't Just Network; Network in the Right Places!

Building a brand-new network from scratch in NYC was daunting, especially without a clear vision of my business. After seven years of speaking Spanish and Portuguese, I had to expertly switch back to English, crafting my messaging in real-time. Finding the right networking groups was challenging at first. Over time, I identified the best circles and events, which also led me to join the Financial Women's Association (FWA). Occasionally, I attended seemingly irrelevant networking events (mainly for entrepreneurs) simply because they seemed fun. After all, you never know who you might meet.

Networking can be a rewarding and enjoyable experience, but it's not always effective for your specific goals. You need to find the right networking circles that align with your objectives.

Here are some suggestions to make networking work for you:

- Research and identify relevant groups: Take time to research and identify networking circles and events that align with your specific professional goals and interests. Don't limit yourself to your industry when looking for organizations and gatherings, especially if your target market is not within your own industry. Attend a variety of events, even those outside your immediate field of interest, to broaden your connections. People know other people...
- Craft and refine your pitch: Develop a clear and engaging pitch (or introduction). Be prepared to experiment with your message. Networking offers you the opportunity to test it, refine it, and make it resonate with your audience, based on feedback and reactions from those you meet.
- Engage actively: Engage actively in conversations and seek out potential contacts who can offer valuable insights or opportunities. Three meaningful connections are usually more valuable than 20 irrelevant or superficial ones.

*

As always, my activities included dance. I've mentioned this before, haven't I? New York City provided a vast array of options, from Salsa and Kizomba to Kompa, traditional and modern African dance styles, and House Dance. Among these, I discovered what would become my favorite: Congolese Ndombolo. But more on that shortly!

Chapter 13:
Dance Is My Life, and My Life Is a Dance

Lessons in Self-Care

When I wasn't darting between networking events, you could find me dancing or taking long walks through Central Park or the city. There were weekends when I would easily walk over 200 blocks. Dancing and walking became my ultimate Manhattan fitness regimen.

Initially, I took numerous dance classes at Equinox, which offered a decent variety of dance options along with other workouts and plenty of yoga classes. However, some of my favorite dance classes were gradually removed. Eventually, I decided to replace my gym membership – despite its convenience with multiple locations throughout the city, saunas, and fully-equipped locker rooms – with frequent dance classes at dedicated dance studios.

On weekends, I started with West African dance classes led by Vado Diomande and other instructors. I loved the live drumming in those classes. Those drums lifted me to new heights every single time. It's no wonder they call drums the "heartbeat of the Earth."

Later, I continued my West African dance journey with Nafisa Shariff in Harlem and shifted my Sunday and Monday focus to Angel Kaba's Afro Urban Street dance classes. Most Sunday afternoons, I'd stroll from the north to the south of Central Park, from my home in Harlem to the dance studio. These walks served as a pre-warm-up and a delightful immersion in nature. They also provided an excellent opportunity to practice my talks for speaking engagements, as I found that walking was the best way for me to rehearse. I was a living walkie-talkie.

Tuesday evenings were dedicated to House dance with Kim Holmes, whose classes were among the sweatiest and most invigorating. Kim's and Angel's classes not only offered physically demanding dance techniques and mentally challenging choreography but also provided excellent cardio, muscle conditioning, and stretching exercises. What I valued most about these sessions was that they included a vigorous warm-up and comprehensive workout, eliminating the need for monotonous gym routines and saving me valuable time. In one of Kim's classes, typically accompanied by canned House music, the Congolese musician Nkumu Katalay joined us with his drum. After class, we walked to the subway together. I had met Nkumu before and attended some of his concerts in Harlem, where his band played primarily Congolese Rumba and Ndombolo. However, apart from one traditional Congolese dance workshop, I had never studied Congolese dance. Nkumu convinced me to take Ndombolo classes, which turned out to be the best thing that could have happened to me. I have a deep love for contemporary Congolese music, which, like Haitian Kompa, instantly touches me at a soul level. You know that feeling when music feels like a caress that moves beyond the senses, below skin level? That's Ndombolo for me.

I began studying Ndombolo with Nkumu and attended all his shows in New York – at the Shrine and Silvana's in Harlem, at concerts in the park or festivals, at LunÀtico in Brooklyn (on my birthday!), at the Museum of Modern Art (MoMA), and more. Wherever he played, I would be there… until March 2020, when everything shut down, and I left New York to escape the restrictive, freedom-curtailing lockdowns. After that, we scheduled online practice sessions to keep the vibe alive. It felt like Ndombolo was somehow in my blood (past life?), though it was challenging to fully grasp the complex rhythm at first, let alone the dance movements. As a side note, if you want to train your thigh muscles, try Ndombolo. It will do the job! Fact is, I still love Ndombolo and always will.

One of the things I also love about New York is the multitude of concerts and festivals in the parks across all boroughs, particularly

Central Park, Prospect Park in Brooklyn, and the smaller parks in Harlem. I had the best time at African and House Dance festivals. The Central Park and Prospect Park Summer Stages brought many beloved artists from overseas, including the iconic Beninese singer Angélique Kidjo and Angolan singer Paulo Flores. Each summer, I'd get the program and add all my favorite shows to my calendar so I wouldn't miss one of them. Summer in New York was truly bombastic.

Leadership Wisdom – Key Takeaways

Do What Makes Your Heart Sing to Stay Fit and Keep Your Vibration High

The most effective fitness regimen for body, mind, and spirit is one that resonates with you, allowing you to disconnect, challenging you both mentally and physically. I often observe people struggling through runs in the park, clearly not enjoying themselves. I tried it a few times myself – living next to Central Park for years made it tempting, but it just wasn't for me. Running leaves me drained quickly. On the contrary, put me in a dance class, and I'll jump around effortlessly, even though it's often more physically demanding.

I can maintain a good pace biking for long stretches, and I love spending four hours walking through the city on weekends or hiking in the mountains. Just don't ask me to run! Sports classes in school were another story. I disliked everything about them. I might have enjoyed handball or basketball if I hadn't always been the last one chosen for the teams, which left me feeling rejected. I struggled with activities like jumping, running, swimming, or gymnastics, all of which were competitive and led to poor grades. Physical education turned me off sports, although I did find joy in skiing and hiking with my dad and siblings. Eventually, I discovered what truly resonated with me: biking, yoga (been doing that on and off), and, above all, dance. Now, at 60, I'm fitter than I was at 20.

If you're struggling to find motivation to exercise, try activities that align with your preferences and bring you joy. Can't decide? A leisurely walk in nature is an excellent starting point. Experiment different options with trial classes at gyms, dance studios, or elsewhere. Some communities even offer free fitness, yoga, or dance classes outdoors during the warmer season. Committing to your health and fitness is an essential part of self-leadership.

Don't have the time? – Then make it! Schedule self-care on your calendar, just like any other important meeting, so it's protected from being booked over.

Consider incorporating it into your morning routine. Personally, I enjoy fitting in a bit of exercise each morning. However, I typically dedicate more time to it in the evening, especially since my dance classes are usually scheduled then, and I can more easily combine bike rides with other leisurely activities. There was a time when I was a member at Equinox, and I would occasionally attend one of their many daytime classes. Ultimately, you need to find what works best for you to ensure you stick with it.

*

The years in New York were slipping by in a blur. Why does time seem to race faster as we get older? Is it just unfair, or have our lives become so overstimulated that we're losing track? Or is the world truly accelerating around us? Perhaps it's a mix of all three. Either way, time was flying by, especially as I ventured on thrilling adventures on a new continent – Africa.

Chapter 14

From the Big Apple to Alkebulan – First Footprints in West Africa

Lessons in Flexibility

Up until 2017, my travels to Africa had been limited to the northern region, specifically Morocco, where I spent a memorable ten days in 2006, visiting some of the country's cultural highlights, traveling from city to city on buses and trains. While my companion indulged in watching soccer games (it was the time of the FIFA World Cup), I found myself unexpectedly winning billiards matches against a local at a nearby bar – a game I hadn't played in decades. But I digress…

In 2017, a dear Cuban friend from Washington D.C., Ana María, introduced me to a contact of hers in Ghana, Steven, who connected us with Princess Asie Ocansey. Princess Asie was organizing a major summit in Accra at the end of July and graciously invited me to speak, along with coaching young women for their upcoming job interviews. Unfortunately, the summit was abruptly canceled, leaving me with booked flights and a cleared calendar, alongside an invitation to speak at the WOVSA Indaba in Johannesburg in August. Determined to contribute, I proceeded with my travels, focusing on preparing these young women for their professional endeavors.

During my stay, I was hosted by a lawyer in Accra who provided me with reasonably priced lodging (which, yes, was supposed to be covered originally, but oh well…) and made it possible for me to see firsthand the transformative impact of coaching these young women. Despite having limited time to explore beyond Accra and Senchi, where I spent a day with Princess Asie, the experience was deeply fulfilling as I witnessed the significant strides the women made and their subsequent success in their interviews. Thanks to Princess Asie's connections, we had the opportunity to meet with various government officials, including the Vice President – at his residence, offering me a unique glimpse into both the formalities of their offices and the dynamics of sponsorship in political circles. And, finally, I was interviewed by journalists for the Ghanaian Goldstreet Business newspaper, which published an article titled "US human resource expert to begin training for one million Ghanaian women," which also included a large photo of Princess Asie and me. All in all, it was a gratifying experience supporting the young women and yet another interesting and multi-faceted learning curve.

Teaching a session at the Africa Internship Academy, where I was invited by Emmanuel Leslie, and meeting his team and some of the participants in the internship program, was another standout experience during my time in Ghana. I spent an entire day there, meeting driven young people with ambitious entrepreneurial plans.

One Sunday afternoon, in a modest neighborhood of central Accra, I had the pleasure of strolling with a new friend who was also staying at the lawyer's house. It was here that I encountered the most incredible fried sweet potatoes of my life, prepared in a large pot by a local woman outside her home, priced at just $0.50. The flavor was unparalleled, distinctly different from any I had tasted before or would ever taste after. What struck me most was her genuine hospitality; she didn't consider charging more just because I was a visitor. This is something I observed throughout my visit to Ghana and pretty much all places in Africa so far – negotiating included in certain situations.

To get around the city, I relied mostly on Uber, occasionally opting for taxis or buses, especially for grocery runs. Some Uber drivers struggled to locate my accommodation, mainly because there was no formal address. I guided them using landmarks like churches, which often led to delays, prompting me to leave with ample time whenever possible.

I had encountered a similar challenge when I first met Princess Asie at her project's home; my Uber driver located her team's office only after calling them, revealing we were in a completely different downtown area. Despite these hurdles, I always managed to reach my destination.

In contrast, Centre for National Culture (a huge arts and crafts market, where you can observe artists and artisans make their products) or the Makola Market (food market) posed no difficulties. Exploring the arts and crafts market was a highlight, where I rediscovered playing the djembe after over a decade, alongside a local craftsman. A visit to Accra would be incomplete without experiencing this colorful market, where you can get an insightful glimpse into the production of the various goods.

Leadership Wisdom – Key Takeaways

Living an Enriching Life Sometimes Requires Flexibility

Traveling in countries that are vastly different to our own allows us to practice flexibility. Being adaptable, being playful with new circumstances, and open to change can lead to a more fulfilling and enriching life. Rigidity or resistance, on the other hand, may hinder personal growth and limit experiences.

Consider where in your life you might be too rigid. Are you restricting yourself with outdated rules? Are you confining yourself within unnecessary limits because you're unwilling to adapt to changes in your environment or to the growth within yourself? Are you inflicting unnecessary pain on self or others by holding onto old resentments instead of showing more flexibility in your relationships? Are you clinging to old habits due to an unwillingness to adapt to your current needs?

These questions may seem challenging or even absurd to you, but I encourage you to reflect on them carefully. By analyzing them thoroughly, you might gain valuable insights that lift your personal growth to a whole new level and propel you into an unprecedented sense of freedom, allowing for a richer and more fulfilling life. Openness to the new will bring a special kind of wealth to your life.

*

When it was time to say goodbye, Princess Asie and her driver took me to the airport. Leaving West Africa so abruptly and without seeing more of Ghana saddened me a bit, but I was also eager for my adventure in the southern reaches of the continent: Johannesburg was next.

Chapter 15
Joburg: From Sandton's Business Vibe to Maboneng's Creative Pulse

Lessons in the Profound Impact of Our Words

Upon landing in Johannesburg, I hopped on the Gautrain to Sandton, where the WOVSA (Women of Value Southern Africa) Indaba was set to take place at the grand Sandton Convention Center. Dimakatso, the conference host, had kindly arranged for my stay at a hotel adjacent to the Convention Center, making everything incredibly convenient. An evening event was also planned at one of the upscale hotels nearby.

The excitement was palpable as I made my way to the venue, eager to make new connections from South Africa and neighboring countries. On a side note, I was thrilled to see my feature in the August edition of Letlotlo magazine, marking my second appearance in the African press. It felt like a significant milestone and added to the thrill of the trip.

The conference itself was a phenomenal experience. I connected with numerous inspiring individuals and made many wonderful new friends, including Lefentse, Barbara, Portia, Masingita, Tintswalo, Nivashnee, Thuto, and Queen Cynthia. On a later visit in 2019, Queen Cynthia even invited me to speak at her coronation. Unfortunately, it was too far from Johannesburg for me to attend, but the invitation alone was a tremendous honor. Isn't it amazing to receive opportunities to speak at our friends' major life events? The WOVSA conference marked my first encounter with South African royals and all the ceremony and protocol surrounding their presence, adding a whole new dimension to my experience.

I was scheduled to teach a 3-hour workshop on the second day of the event. However, due to longer-than-expected speeches and panels, the program changed, and – as so many others – I found myself on a panel instead. Despite the shift, I still managed to give a shorter presentation. As I mentioned in the previous chapter, sometimes life requires us to be flexible to succeed.

What deeply touched me that day was during the Q&A portion of my presentation a lady stood up to take the microphone. She shared that one specific thing I'd said had completely changed her perspective on what she could achieve in her life. She expressed newfound confidence that, as a result, she would be able to elevate her business and life to new heights. Moments like these truly make my heart sing.

I also took advantage of this visit to reconnect with Nonkululeko (Nku), a friend I'd met at a dance class in New York City, and finally meet Amina and Wayne, business friends I'd only known virtually. Amina graciously invited me to her home, where we enjoyed a lovely dinner with her family. While chatting with Nku over lunch, we decided to attend a hot yoga class one Sunday morning. Running late, we were stopped by the traffic police for speeding. However, Nku skillfully talked us out of a fine, and we were soon back on our way.

During my stay, I also attended a smaller conference featuring many amazing speakers, including university professor Milena as well as Arthie, the latter being connected with another business friend of mine, Matt. One Sunday afternoon, Matt took me to Maboneng Precinct to Market on Main, an incredible food market housed in an old industrial building surrounded by a complex of restaurants and small art shops. On a side note, Maboneng is the Sesotho word for "Place of Light."

We followed our food sampling with an open-air Kizomba/Salsa party, so I even got to dance a little. Arthie and her husband joined us later, and we ventured over to a small hole-in-the-wall spot to eat some chicken before taking the elevator up to the Living Room, a resto-bar on Kruger Street, where the prevailing music style was House. I immediately fell in love with the artistic neighborhood of Maboneng, which boasts a large selection of restaurants and bars, apart from the weekend street market with all sorts of arts and crafts and lots of outdoor partying. It's an inner-city revitalized district with a wealth of painted murals and industrial buildings converted into apartments for locals, as well as some Airbnbs for tourists, including the Curiocity Backpackers on Fox St. With all the artists selling their work and the many art-covered walls of many of its streets, this urban precinct is a hub of creativity.

The vibrancy and creativity of Maboneng left a lasting impression on me, making it one of the highlights of my visit. I decided that if I ever returned to Johannesburg, Maboneng Precinct would be my home base. True to my word, it became my go-to place whenever I stayed in Joburg, sometimes for a month or longer.

Leadership Wisdom – Key Takeaways

Unlock the Impact of Your Message and Transform Lives

When that woman stood up and shared how one particular statement from my presentation had changed her perspective, I realized the profound impact of speaking at that conference. It made traveling there so worth it. And it marked a pivotal moment that underscored the power of our words.

What message burns within you, waiting to be shared with the world? Consider the profound potential in your voice! Just imagine how many lives you could change!

Now is your moment to step forward and share your unique gift with the world! If hesitation holds you back – perhaps due to nerves about speaking in public – explore my book *Speak Up, Stand Out and Shine* on Amazon. It's packed with practical tips and techniques to help you find the courage and confidence to stand before your audience and deliver your message effectively. There are people who need to hear what you have to say.

*

I knew this was not going to be my last time in this country. I had made far too many friends this time around, and there was also dancing for me in Joburg, making an extended stay even more appealing. Up in the clouds on my flight home, I was already scheming up a reason for my next visit.

Chapter 16

Sharp Sharp and the Robots in Mzansi

Lessons in Elevating Travel Experiences and Trusting Intuition

On my next visit, I found my first Airbnb in Maboneng on Main Street, where I met a new friend and neighbor, Asanda. We'd often relax around the small fountain in the patio of the zebra-pattern-painted building. Given the somewhat lax security in that building, I was always vigilant. So, when I woke up one night to the unmistakable sound of someone fiddling with my door lock, a chill ran down my spine. My heart pounded as I mustered the courage to approach the door. Trying to steady my shaking voice, I imitated a gruff, male tone and demanded to know who was there. The seconds stretched into an eternity before a sheepish voice on the other side revealed the truth – it was just another Airbnb guest who had mistaken my apartment for theirs.

Apart from this brief incident, my studio apartment, decorated in a charming safari style, was delightful, but it wasn't available for my entire one-month stay. The owner referred me to Kgosietsile's place on Fox Street. From the window of that studio, I could see a message on the exterior wall of a neighboring building that said, "I love your work." It felt like a personal note from the Universe, affirming that my message was resonating with my audiences in the city. The Universe loves to send us messages, doesn't it?

Kgosi later became a dear friend and client. Talk about the Universe conspiring! I ended up staying at his Airbnb twice, in a massive industrial building with old elevators that, though trendy, were always slow and often out of order. Nevertheless, I loved that place! Once, when Kgosi's apartment wasn't available, I booked a stay with an acquaintance of his in the same building. That place had become my second home in Jozi, just steps away from all my favorite spots in Maboneng: the dance joint for Sunday afternoons, the Congolese Bertrand Café up the street (my favorite hangout where I'd always meet new friends and run into local buddies like Senzo, who owned the Love Revo restaurant and bike rental across the street).

It was also where I met Mabila, who worked in high-end Airbnb property management, and Reggie, an amazing painter who achieved international fame. I was invited to visit his Maboneng studio a few times to admire his art and help him transport some of his canvases to Brooklyn for an exhibition on my way back from Joburg to New York in 2019.

Occasionally, Bertrand's would have a DJ who'd play mostly House (South African style, which is my preferred), and the sidewalk in front of the restaurant would turn into the dance floor for cool parties.

My friends, including Portia, Barbara, and Lefentse, who lived in other parts of the city and Durban, were always happy to spend time in Maboneng. We'd often meet there, though occasionally I'd also go to Sandton, Rosebank Mall, or other parts of town to see some of the lovely people I'd met at that very first conference where I was speaking. Once, I even ventured out to Pretoria for a lady who wanted to discuss training for women in local government, which, however, never came about as there were certain requirements for providers of such services, which I – as a white woman – didn't meet.

Sbusisiwe, Yoliswa, and Toni are some other names that come to mind when I think of South Africa. Meeting up with these remarkable ladies to chat about business, projects, and causes often turned into an opportunity to enjoy a delightful lunch or dinner together. It was always a refreshing break from my usual desk work.

At one point, I was booked at a Sandton hotel again for a few nights when BCG hired me to teach a workshop to a group of their employees at a beautiful venue. When I first visited the office, I couldn't find the address right away, so I asked a security guard in the street. He pointed up the street and instructed me to "turn right at the robot." Desperately searching for a robot, I couldn't see one. I asked again to ensure I'd understood him correctly. He stared at me incredulously, not understanding why I didn't see the robot. I looked at him, then back in the direction he was pointing, probably with big question marks in my eyes. Not wanting to ask a third time, I thanked him and walked up to the traffic light, turned right and right again, and eventually found the building entrance. Only later did I learn that "robot" means "traffic light" in South Africa, something I must have missed during my first visit for some reason.

On another occasion, I decided to revisit the chicken place on Kruger St. where we'd eaten during my first visit to Maboneng. As I entered, the guy selling food greeted me with a spirited "shop shop." I initially thought, "Hold on, I just got here! Let me take my time deciding." Despite my bemusement, I greeted him politely, placed my order, paid, and left. To my surprise, I encountered the same "shop shop" greeting in other shops and cafés around town. Eventually, I realized they were actually saying "sharp sharp," which loosely translates to "what's up?" or "how are you?" Language truly can be fascinating! By the way, did you know that when South Africans say, "you look smart," they're not commenting on your intelligence? It's their way of saying you're well-dressed or look elegant.

While Johannesburg isn't the safest city for leisurely strolls, I managed to enjoy some wonderful walks around Braamfontein ("Braamies") and of course Maboneng. I immersed myself in the vibrant murals, visited a few small museums, and explored eclectic bars. Over time, I learned where the safer areas were within the Maboneng precinct. For basic groceries like water, eggs, bread, and wine, I shopped locally. Anything more sophisticated required venturing outside the area, though Maboneng had its share of excellent restaurants to dine at.

Given the distance to the Gautrain station in Parktown, I usually relied on Uber to get there or to other places that weren't served by the subway. However, one memorable day, I took a "taxi" (a small van, similar to the ones used in Rio de Janeiro, in addition to regular buses) in Jeppestown to a shopping center with my new friend Hloni. Normally cautious about traveling alone in Johannesburg due to unfamiliarity, unlike Rio de Janeiro where I navigated confidently, I preferred not to risk ending up in the wrong neighborhood by myself. Safety first, even when exploring an intriguing city like Jozi!

Having said that, I discovered that Thursday nights in Maboneng meant night bike rides organized by Senzo, the owner of the Love Revo resto. These rides became a highlight of my week. Joined by locals and occasional visitors from abroad, we set off in different directions each week. Our first ride took us down Commissioner Street, eventually leading to a biker's home in Kensington. Another time, we ventured to a secluded rooftop atop a parking garage, a hidden spot only a local could unveil. From there, we navigated through downtown's dimly lit streets, catching glimpses of people squatting in former industrial buildings turned into makeshift shelters. Parts of the ride were brisk and cautious, swiftly biking through risky areas where stopping was ill-advised – especially hoping no punctures would force us to stop. A flat tire in one specific place we passed through would not have been my favorite type of adventure. Finally, we'd reach an area of trendy bars, each with its own distinctive charm. We chose the most spectacular one for a break before heading back to our departure point. While the guys savored house-specialty cocktails, I preferred some delicious South African wine.

Another memorable bike ride led us along a deserted section of highway, normally bustling with traffic. We also ventured into other enigmatic corners of the city, including a visit to the home of the owner of Curiocity Backpackers. These rides were undoubtedly among the highlights of my time in Joburg, together with another bike excursion during the day, more of which later.

On Sunday afternoons, I frequented the outdoor bar Matt had introduced me to in the past, where Kizomba, Semba, and Salsa dancing awaited. It was here that I met exceptional dancers from South Africa and Angola. Those Sunday afternoons were my dancer's paradise! During some of my later Joburg visits, Faye Baba, a neighbor from the building, or Hloni, would sometimes join me on my dance or rooftop outings.

One evening, as I strolled back from dinner, I encountered Zebe, a Zimbabwean Rastafarian selling belts, earrings, and other artisanal items alongside a younger companion. Our conversation meandered through various topics until it settled on dance. Zebe mentioned his work with the people at the Drill Hall, a vast former military facility transformed into a hub where artists and craftsmen lived and worked, creating everything from bags to jewelry. He was also teaching a group of teenagers to dance at that place.

"You must come visit!" Zebe insisted before gifting me a pair of earrings. Intrigued, I inquired among friends about the Drill Hall and planned to Uber there. The response was skeptical: "Good luck finding a driver willing to go." Since Zebe didn't own a phone, coordinating our visit relied on reaching out through mutual friends like Karabo.

Eventually, I connected with Zebe again and proposed he accompany me. To my surprise, he showed up on the agreed-upon day, despite his spontaneous lifestyle. I'm not sure what made me trust this person, except that my intuition allowed me to. Intuition is priceless when we care to listen to it. Together, we walked from Fox Street in Maboneng to Drill Hall, located in Hillbrow next to the Taxi Rank. The route took us through unfamiliar streets not recommended for outsiders. I'm certain I wouldn't have made it through unscathed on my own.

I will never forget this walk; specific scenes remain vividly etched in my mind. It's hard to describe my experience as most of my impressions flowed through my emotional channels. While I absorbed everything with my eyes and ears, much of it was felt energetically.

I do know that I wouldn't have wanted to walk this route alone, which in itself speaks volumes, as I'm not generally risk averse. It remains a precious and special memory, despite witnessing horrifying drug abuse on the sidewalks. I noticed that my chaperon was constantly alert, always on the lookout. Once a clearly troubled individual approached us in a slightly menacing way, but Zebe quickly put him in his place with a few firm words. This brief encounter was the only incident, and it was swiftly handled by my companion.

With Zebe's familiarity with locals along our route, we made it through safely, though discreetly, mindful not to attract too much attention, which was pretty much impossible for a tourist. We reached our destination safe and sound, with me being extremely grateful for Zebe's guidance and local knowledge that made the excursion possible.

As we approached the Drill Hall area, we passed by a group of guys washing cars at a car wash. When we paused to greet them, they expressed their surprise and appreciation, saying, "Wow, it's so great that you're coming here. There's never really any people from outside the area who come see us here." Continuing on our path to the Drill Hall, we bought some fruit and greeted more of Zebe's acquaintances along the way, including a lovely lady selling soap. Eventually, we arrived and stepped inside.

Zebe took me on a tour of the ground floor, where large paintings were exhibited in the rooms and hallways, waiting for their completion. We strolled through the outdoor area with a skating rink and then entered a side building where several artists shared rooms, some of whom were asleep. Next, we visited a hall where a group of guys put on a spontaneous dance show for me. I tried to follow their moves, but their choreography was too advanced for me to grasp so quickly – it was a lot of fun nonetheless! Finally, we ascended to the first floor of the main building, a vast hall with people crafting handbags, earrings, fabric and leather items, and wire figurines, mostly from recycled materials, such as leftover pieces of leather. On the balcony, a heap of old tires awaited transformation into sandals. As a parting gift, I received a beautifully crafted handbag, and on our way out, I met a talented artisan named Elvis, who fashioned colorful flowers from beads. What an extraordinary experience!

When it was time to bid farewell, Karabo (who was hugely into fashion) decided to walk back with us. Along the way, we encountered a couple of Zebe's Rasta friends selling items on the sidewalk. They treated me to an impromptu "Rasta hip-hop" song, and some of the guys formed a protective circle around me so I could record it on my phone. It was one of those "extra-special" moments.

Upon returning to Maboneng, Zebe surprised me by revealing a huge pair of scissors tucked up his sleeve – his discreet self-defense measure. Although I had been aware of potential danger, Zebe's preparedness underscored the reality of the environment and his determination to ensure our safety.

That evening, we joined Senzo's bike ride group once again, which led us to the Backpackers' owner's home with its stunning view over the city – the perfect conclusion to an unforgettable day. But it was more than just that. It was another serendipitous coincidence: I had suggested to Zebe to discuss potential business with this man. The Backpackers attracted many potential customers for the Drill Hall products. I recounted my day excursion and Zebe's story to him. Unfortunately, I never managed to reconnect with Zebe, who, according to one of his friends, had been laying low for some unknown reason. If only we had found a way to communicate without relying on his cellphone, synchronicity might have been on his side that day.

Six and a half months in South Africa can't possibly fit into just one chapter, so join me in the next chapter for more adventures in Mzansi!

Leadership Wisdom – Key Takeaways

Talk to Locals for That Special Travel Experience

When traveling, engaging with locals opens doors to unforgettable experiences and invaluable insights into different cultures and walks of life. These interactions often lead to moments you wouldn't encounter through traditional tourist services. However, while "doing like the locals do" can enhance your journey, it's essential to exercise discretion and caution where needed. What may be safe and enriching in one context could pose risks in another. Finding the right balance between exploration and caution is key. Don't let yourself guided by FOMO (fear of missing out) alone. Trusting your intuition and evaluating situations carefully is useful for these decisions. While many locals are welcoming and trustworthy, exercising prudence ensures you maximize your experience without compromising safety.

By the way, thrilling travel doesn't have to break the bank. I often hear people say, "I'd love to travel like you, but I can't afford it." The truth is, I often spent less money on the road than I did living in NYC. For a time, I even had a flexible arrangement with my NYC landlord, who charged me little to nothing when I wasn't using the apartment. This was only possible with a less formal lease, but my point is: Think creatively and you will discover a way.

Listen to Your Intuition to Gauge People and Situations

When we make new connections, we can't always know right away whether they have our best interests in mind and whether we should trust them or not. Learning to use our intuition is priceless in these situations.

The same applies to interpersonal relationships in business. In an earlier chapter, I shared an example of when I did not listen to my intuitive voice, which led to an extremely painful disappointment by my business partner. Something inside of me was stirring, but I didn't care to pay attention to it. I wanted it to not be true.

I encourage you to connect with your heart whenever in doubt about someone's intentions or about a decision you must make. Don't know how to do this? Check out my YouTube channel, where you can find great tips, or reach out directly to me and let's have a chat!

*

With every departure from South Africa, I left richer in friends and experience, my heart filled with more reasons to return. While Johannesburg was my primary base, I also stepped outside to visit other places, like Durban, Cape Town, and White River/Mpumalanga. More about that shortly…

Chapter 17

South Africa Continued: More Encounters and Poked by an Elephant

Lessons in Appreciation and Generosity

There was a time when I actively reached out to people in several African countries simply by contacting them online. Jenna Clifford, the renowned jewelry designer, was one such person. To my surprise, she agreed to meet, though she was living on her farm in Mpumalanga and only occasionally visiting Johannesburg. She suggested I meet with Sonja, the General Manager of her Flagship Design Studio in Morningside, first.

As is customary in South Africa, Sonja greeted me with a bottle of chilled white wine. I left with another bottle of wine and a beautiful wine stopper as a gift, and a promise that Sonja would take me to Jenna's farm along with another staff member, where they'd soon be filming commercials. Sonja kept her promise! A few days later, we met up to drive to White River, staying at a nearby house where they had rented some rooms.

Before settling in, we visited Jenna's extensive property. On the way to the farmhouse, we strolled through a stable with horses and a donkey. Outside, more horses grazed alongside other animals. A group of huge dogs followed us everywhere, most of them peaceful and sweet. However, one had a bit of an ill temper and liked to pester us occasionally. I love dogs, but some can be a little unpredictable or sneaky, and this one certainly was.

Jenna was not just a talented jewelry designer but also an amazing cook. She had prepared a delicious vegetable lasagna, which she planned to bake later. For now, she opened a bottle of white wine. As we sipped our glasses, we chatted about work – hers, mine, Sonja's, and the upcoming shoot for the new commercials. Jenna's strong personality and generosity made for an intensely interesting day.

One thing I quickly learned in Mzansi is that some South Africans drink white wine like water. While I enjoy a good glass of wine with dinner and can appreciate a fine vintage, I simply couldn't keep up with many of them, including these ladies!

In the following days, we visited another one of Jenna's properties – a beautifully furnished mansion she rented out for events like retreats. We also explored some nearby natural beauties before it was time to return to the city, and my "travel package" even included a relaxing massage at the property we were staying at.

One time, I took a bike ride through Soweto with my friend Barbara. I had been to Soweto before, but only for a short visit around Mandela House, part of a quick tour organized by Dimakatso, the WOVSA conference host. This bike ride, though also guided, was a completely different experience. We covered a much larger area of Soweto, explored various neighborhoods, chatted with residents, and even tasted some of the distinct beer of a local tribe.

In September 2019, I made another trip to Soweto, this time with Lefentse. We ventured to the lively Sunday afternoon party scene, where we also met one of her colleagues, his friend, and Nobayeni, a local dancer I had previously encountered in Maboneng. We spent the day sharing beers, exchanging stories, and capturing some wild photos together. It was a relaxed and groovy Sunday afternoon.

During one particular visit to South Africa, I flew down to Cape Town, following invitations from two friends: Inet, whom I'd met through an online networking group, and Christo, whose Brooklyn party I'd attended before he moved back to his home country.

Inet was kind enough to pick me up at the airport and drive us to her home in the Western Cape. With her, I had the best fish and chips ever at Fish Hoek, and we also explored some nearby nature gems in her car. For my second destination, Christo's house, I took a cab with a friendly driver who happened to be a tour guide. He stopped at some amazing vantage points along the way.

One morning, Christo and I got up extra early to hike up Table Mountain, where we were rewarded with breathtaking views of Cape Town and the surrounding areas. Although the hike was relatively short compared to the mountains in my Bavarian home, we wanted to reach the top before it got too hot. Christo also took me to some of the most beautiful Stellenbosch wineries and vineyards, where we tasted exquisite wines and food.

If you ever travel to Cape Town, I highly recommend getting a 2-day ticket for the hop-on hop-off tourist bus. It's an excellent option as the bus takes you far outside the city on a long route that would be too much to cover in one day if you want to truly enjoy the experience. You can hop off at the large botanical garden, along the many beaches, or for a walking tour through a township. As a very independent traveler, I usually avoid tourist groups and voyeuristic tours, but I decided to do the township stop because the guide was waiting at the stop and no one else was getting off. This meant she wouldn't earn any tips if I didn't go with her, and it gave me the chance to have a deeper conversation than walking with a group of tourists. It felt more like strolling with a friend, which was nice. We bought some water and snacks at a local shop, and she showed me around, sharing stories about the township's residents. By the time I left, we'd become friends.

The botanical garden stop was a must, and I loved sitting on the open top deck of the bus, enjoying the scenery. It was a real treat. I initially bought a 1-day ticket, thinking I'd be back much sooner, but I realized the ride was long and there were more interesting stops to explore. So, I went back and added the second day, which was 100% worth it!

After spending New Year's in Cape Town (at a rather dull party with oldies music completely outside my range of taste), it was time to head back to Johannesburg for a few days before catching another flight to Durban. In Durban, I initially stayed at a small B&B in a predominantly Indian neighborhood, before moving in with Lefentse, who awaited me in a beautiful apartment on the beach just north of Durban. Fun fact: the area had lots of monkeys, so we had to be careful to always close the windows when we were out, or they would get in and wreak havoc, as they had once done at my friend's house, eating most of her groceries and breaking bottles.

On my first day with Lefentse, we had lunch in the Harbor area. Afterward, she went to her office, and I continued exploring different neighborhoods of Durban on foot and by bus before heading back north.

One especially memorable night was spent at The Chairman, a renowned and beautifully decorated jazz bar. The owner, an architect, had designed it impeccably. I was treated to a marvelous live performance by the local NAT Jazz Band, which consisted of several generations of musicians. I could have watched and listened to their music all night, despite not being a huge jazz fan or connoisseur. The only other jazz performance that had moved me this much was by John Lurie & the Lounge Lizards, who I'd seen live in Munich in my early twenties, even though it was a completely different style.

While in Durban, I also visited a youth training center founded by Zondwa Mandela and his team, whom I had met in New York and with whom I'd had a Zoom meeting to discuss potential collaboration. Although I did meet with the managing team of the center, the timing wasn't right for us to move forward, as they were in the midst of other programs. We still had an enriching meeting, though, and it was an interesting experience to learn about the center's activities.

At a café of a local shopping mall, I enjoyed a coffee with Senamile Masango, a renowned nuclear scientist whom I had been introduced to by my friend Ana María from D.C. Our conversation was delightful, and Senamile later invited me to speak at one of her online events.

One of my highlights in Durban was visiting PheZulu Safari Park and Natal Lion Park near Pietermaritzburg. I arranged for a driver and guide to pick me up on one of my last mornings in Durban.

Entering Natal Lion Park was an adventure in itself: we had to drive into a large enclosure, where the gate behind us closed before the one in front opened. In our small car, which felt like a toy compared to the majestic lions around us, I was captivated by a pride of what seemed like giant lions to me, lounging in the midday sun. They were stretched out lazily in the sun at first, but soon enough, they started to stand and display their impressive forms. It was exhilarating to be so close to these regal animals, though we stayed safely inside the car with the windows up to ensure their comfort (and ours). It was clear that moving cautiously and heeding expert advice was crucial when in the presence of such powerful creatures.

In an adjacent park, we encountered a man with a tame elephant. I was given the chance to feed the elephant some snacks, which it grabbed eagerly from my hand. When the bag was empty and I turned around, the elephant nudged me with its trunk, almost toppling me over. It was a vivid jolt to the senses that caught me by surprise, leaving an indelible mark on my memory.

The Safari Park visit was equally memorable. We spent quite a while searching for giraffes until we finally spotted them in the distance. As we got closer, some of them seemed to be stretching and bending in what looked like a yoga session. It was a delightful and whimsical moment that capped off an fabulous experience.

Before leaving Durban, I had the pleasure of meeting Gcina Mhlope through my friend Lefentse. Gcina, a renowned author, playwright, performer, and storyteller, leads a remarkable literacy project that has touched countless lives. During one of our meetings, we exchanged books, and I was struck by her presence and passion.

Her extraordinary storytelling skills made her a perfect fit for an international women's conference I would speak at in Johannesburg in 2019. I introduced her to the event, and it was a privilege to see her take the stage and share her wisdom and voice. But I'm skipping ahead again... More about that trip later.

Leadership Wisdom – Key Takeaways

Showing Appreciation for Every Experience Brings Abundance

Abundance comes in many shapes and forms. One of them is wisdom and growth. Recognizing and valuing each experience enriches not just our perception of our own lives, but also our understanding, and it informs better decision-making. By appreciating both the small moments and significant events, we can develop a more nuanced perspective and enhance our ability to navigate future challenges.

Also, appreciation tells the Universe that this is what you want more of, and the Universe is always happy to deliver according to the vibration you emanate and the signals you send out to it.

- Acknowledge unique contributions. When someone goes out of their way to help or share something special with you, acknowledge their effort and express your gratitude. This not only strengthens your relationships but also fosters a positive and supportive environment. Whether it's someone's culinary skills or the local insight you gain from conversations in a different culture, make it a point to acknowledge and appreciate the unique contributions of each experience. Recognize what each interaction brought to your growth and express your gratitude to those who made it special.
- Capture and reflect on memorable moments. Just as you take the time to savor your unique experiences (such as the beauty of Table Mountain or the atmosphere of The Chairman jazz bar), capture these moments in a journal. Reflecting on these memories helps you cherish the richness of each experience and can offer valuable insights for future endeavors.

Cultivating a Spirit of Generosity Always Pays Off

I've always found Africans to be profoundly generous wherever I travel. Though my suitcase may be too small to fit all the physical gifts I receive, there's always ample room in my heart for the intangible ones.

Embracing generosity and reciprocity fosters stronger connections and enhances collaborative efforts. By giving and receiving openly, we build trust and create a positive environment where others are motivated to reciprocate.

- Embrace local customs and hospitality: Reciprocating these gestures demonstrates respect and fosters deeper connections. For instance, bringing a small gift (it could be your book) or contributing a session, like I have often done (it doesn't have to be anything material) or simply showing appreciation for local traditions can build goodwill and enhance relationships.

- Be open to unplanned opportunities: Your willingness to join people to explore unexpected activities like an activity with a friend that means a lot to them, or an impromptu teaching session shows your value of flexibility and openness. Approach new experiences and unplanned opportunities with a positive attitude. This openness can lead to enriching encounters and build stronger bonds with those you meet, and it will reward you with unforgettable memories.

- Remember that to receive is to give, and to give is to receive. If you reject a gift, you deprive the other person from giving (and therefore, from receiving the satisfaction that comes from it).

*

As my time in South Africa was coming to an end, I had just a few days left in Johannesburg and was eager to catch another Sunday dance afternoon. The two months had flown by in the blink of an eye, and it was time to head back to the freezing New York winter.

Chapter 18
A New Era of Exploration: Setting Out as a Wandering Gypsy

Lessons in the Power of Words and Connections

In the summer of 2019, I kicked off a new chapter, leaving my Harlem apartment behind to fully dive into a life of relentless exploration. With a packed schedule ahead, my odyssey began with speaking engagements at a SHRM conference in Phoenix, Arizona, followed by a gig at an international conference in Johannesburg. From there, I headed to Maryland for a keynote at a law firm retreat, then to Germany to reconnect with family. I returned briefly to New York City for a summit before setting off for two exhilarating months in East Africa, immersing myself in the cultures of Uganda and Rwanda.

At the time, I didn't realize that this nomadic adventure would extend beyond the year I had initially planned. I had already lined up speaking engagements in Kansas, Hawaii, Kenya, England, Nigeria, South Africa, and yes, also New York City... all the way up until September 2020. Later, I added gigs in East Africa – Kigali, Kampala, and Nairobi, some of which were meant to become long-term collaborations.

However, after March 2020, all these plans were canceled due to the imposed lockdown and travel restrictions. I managed to escape the lockdown just before it tightened its grip, intuitively grasping some of what was ahead. And I wasn't stopped from traveling – just not to the destinations originally planned... and fighting for my basic human right to breathe with airport and airline staff on the ground and in the air.

Back to September 2019! Shortly after returning from Arizona, I boarded a plane to Johannesburg to speak at the Female Wave of

Change (FWoC)[2] international conference as well as at a Data Science Academy event for entrepreneurs and possibly more places. When I arrived at O.R. Tambo International Airport, I called an Uber to take me to my Airbnb in Maboneng. Exhausted from the long journey from New York, I sank into the back seat, eager to freshen up and grab a bite at one of my favorite spots on Fox Street.

To my surprise, the driver, a Zimbabwean, informed me he wasn't sure if he could safely take me to Maboneng. He explained that there had been violent protests and xenophobic attacks in Jeppestown and potentially in Maboneng itself. He turned on the radio to catch any updates. The news was alarming: trucks on the road to Durban were being set on fire, and there were attacks on foreigners and foreign-owned businesses, particularly targeting Nigerians, but also foreigners from other places, in Johannesburg.

The roads were chaotic, with truck drivers confused and traffic jams in areas marked "high-crime," where we'd usually avoid to stop, which wasn't possible today due to the chaos. It was an eerie ride as we navigated through these zones. Thankfully, we made it safely, but as we approached Main Street in Maboneng, we saw protesters with sticks on a parallel street. My driver, almost panicking, asked if we should stop or continue. I urged him to keep going. He overtook the line of cars in front of us and sped to our destination on Fox Street.

He quickly dropped me and my bags off on the sidewalk and drove off as fast as he could. Considering the situation, I couldn't blame him – Zimbabweans were also targets in the unrest, accused of taking local jobs. I hurriedly dragged my two bags inside the building, only to learn that my apartment wouldn't be ready for another hour – not the best news after a flight from New York! When I finally got access to my studio, I quickly took a shower and tried to decide what to do next.

Feeling extremely hungry, I noticed all the usually bustling restaurants on Fox Street were closed, except for a pizza joint that

---

[2] I left this organization in 2020 due to ideological differences

belonged to a small movie theater in the same building. I slipped out the front door and into the adjacent entrance. Shortly after, the noise of the protests resumed outside, and the owners quickly locked the door as men with big sticks and grim faces walked by.

As I waited for my pizza, I met some funky new friends and had a surprisingly fun time, despite my sleepiness. Eventually, I fell into bed, exhausted but relieved to be safe... for now.

On Saturday, as things seemed to have calmed down and restaurants started opening up again, I met two local friends for a photo shoot, one of them being Karabo. For the shoot, we wandered along many of the amazing murals in the Precinct, capturing beautiful moments that day and just having a great time. It took a few days until I received the photos, and they are still among my favorite of all photo shoots I've ever done.

Sunday afternoons were reserved for dancing at the outdoor bar down the street. You may remember that I'd mentioned it before: A charming complex that housed a food market in an indoor parking area, an art gallery, and several arts and crafts shops, all centered around a large interior patio with stairs leading up to the dance venue.

That Sunday, I was eagerly getting ready to head over and dance with some of my favorite partners. Dance shoes were already in my bag. Around 2:30pm, I heard loud noises outside. Looking out the window, I saw street vendors, artists, and artisans hastily packing up their beautiful pieces displayed on the sidewalk. In the other direction, a long caravan of men with sticks and threatening expressions marched down the street. So much for dancing that day – everything shut down again, including all the restaurants and shops.

The following week, I had a meeting scheduled for Thursday night, meaning I'd miss the usual Thursday night bike tour. I contacted Senzo, the tour organizer, to see if there was another day we could go. He typically didn't run tours on other days, but he offered to take me on a ride to check out what had happened with the Nigerian stores along Roberts Avenue affected by the xenophobic attacks. I agreed, and we set off, riding past burned-down car and tire shops. The scene was devastating, resembling a war zone, with destruction targeted specifically at Nigerian small business owners.

We continued riding until we reached a lovely restaurant with a cozy and unique patio, which included a small bus turned into an additional seating area for guests. It was a very special place indeed.

Our outing ran later than expected, and without lights on our bikes, we had to call an Uber to take us back. The car that arrived was too small for our bikes, but with patience and dexterity, the driver managed to fit them in by removing one tire. It took about 15 minutes, a feat I couldn't imagine happening with an Uber driver in New York City. I was relieved and grateful when it all worked out.

Because of traces of the unrest still flaring up here and there, I felt compelled to move to different neighborhood, closer to the conference venue, The Wanderers Club in Fairway, as it wasn't guaranteed that I'd be able to get out of Maboneng in the mornings for an event that stretched over several days. I found a convenient Airbnb in Sandton.

The conference was an incredible opportunity to forge new connections with inspiring women. I met powerhouse Asnath, who quickly became a close friend, and Mmahlapa – together, we showed off some Afrobeat dance moves. I reconnected with Tebello from a previous Johannesburg visit and met Khomotso, the fashion queen, and Paballo, with whom I later enjoyed a rich conversation over tasty lunch. The list of remarkable women I encountered included Cynthia, Josefina, Yvonne, Thekla, Mellany, and many more.

I was thrilled to offer complimentary tickets to my local friends Barbara, Faye, and Hloni, who themselves made some wonderful new connections. One of them resulted in a long-term mentorship that led to an entirely new career, culminating in the authorship of a book.

During this visit, I was also slated to speak at an entrepreneurial event with Renée, a partner I had previously worked with on a specific topic, and with whom I had given a presentation for Dow Jones in NYC. At the event, we met two Angolan friends – one of them, Zee, still stays in touch to this day – and one night, we all went out together, along with Renée's boyfriend. They even joined me one Sunday afternoon at Bertrand's in Maboneng, where we danced a few Kizombas.

While in Johannesburg, my schedule was always packed with meetings and exciting encounters. One standout was with Yolanda from On Cue, who invited me to visit her institute in Midrand. She and her team were teaching young media and film professionals to be "on cue," always ready to speak at the right moment. I was set for a quick session with them – just a short-term call, but why not? It was a lovely day, and once our study time was up, we enjoyed a braai (barbecue) lunch together in the garden.

Another call came from Milena, a professor at the School of Tourism and Hospitality at the University of Johannesburg. I'd met her during one of the events on my first-ever visit. She invited me to teach a session on inclusive leadership for first-year students the next day. It wasn't a paid gig, and it was very short-term, but she offered to pick me up and I managed to make the schedule work, so I agreed.

Teaching the session was challenging in several ways. First, technology: It took us a while to get the projector working. Without the presentation, conveying the content meaningfully would have been tough. Second, this was the first and only session on leadership these students had ever had. Lastly, there was a small group of students sitting in the last row who seemed disinterested and overly "chill." Engaging everyone would be a challenge.

The hall was filled with first-year students and four professors. I decided to start the conversation from the audience's point of view: "What's special or different about you? And why is this of value?" By making it about them, I hoped to engage them right away. This tactic (together with bringing some high-vibe energy) worked great. When I asked for volunteers to come to the front for a fun exercise, both one of the shyest students and the "coolest" guy from the back row volunteered. We all had a blast together.

Milena had ordered sandwiches and other snacks, organizing a little get-together to round off the event. One student came up to me and said, "This was the best lecture I've ever had so far." (It wasn't really a lecture but rather an interactive session, but he was used to the word "lecture.") Another student later emailed me saying, "Thank you so much for coming to teach us. You made me see that I have worth, that I am okay the way I am, and there is no reason to hide who I am." Her message literally brought tears to my eyes. Sometimes, it's amazing what a deep impact words can have…

This reminds me of what Kgosi, my former Airbnb host and client, once said to me: "You are one of the highlights of the past decade." Having a positive impact in people's lives means the world to me. Lunch or dinner conversations with Kgosi were always special occasions. I regret that we can't have them more often, though we do still check in from time to time. It's wonderful to have a symbiotic business relationship where we are mutual clients.

Another memorable encounter was with Kimaany Kimaany, a reggae musician from Cameroon, who was in Johannesburg for a gig and dining with one of his business contacts next to my table one night. We had a great chat, and he gave me his CD. There's something about Maboneng that makes it effortlessly easy to make new friends.

Leadership Wisdom – Key Takeaways

Words Matter – They Can Change Lives

Words hold the power to profoundly impact others, often more deeply than we realize. The acknowledgements I received from my speaking engagements in South Africa and beyond testify to how a simple statement or question can shift someone's perspective and transform their belief in what they can achieve.

This serves as a powerful reminder to use our words wisely and to share the messages that others may need to hear.

As a leader, mastering the art of communication is crucial. It's essential for building functional, cohesive, and happy teams; conveying your vision; gaining buy-in for your projects; and successfully representing your division, organization, or cause.

Reflect on your own communication skills:

- What areas need improvement?
- Are there gaps you need to fill?
- Can you navigate conversations smoothly with your team, top management, clients, and other stakeholders?
- Do you dread difficult conversations or conveying unpopular messages?

Now is the time to enhance your communication skills. Use your words to inspire, motivate, and lead effectively. The impact you can have is immeasurable.

The methods and tools of Conversational Intelligence (C-IQ)® can help. They have allowed many of my clients to enhance their communication skills and become more proficient communicators.

Sometimes, Our Role in People's Lives is Being a Bridge

I am known as a connector, a bridge-builder. There's immense satisfaction in bringing people together for mutual benefit, whether it's introducing potential business partners, clients, or mentors. It's about creating opportunities for growth, collaboration, and shared success.

Think about the people in your network. Who can you be a bridge for? Who can you introduce that might spark a transformative relationship?

- Identify potential connections: Look around your circle. Who has complementary skills or goals? Who could benefit from getting to know each other?
- Take action: Reach out to these individuals. Share why you think they should connect and how they can help each other.
- Follow up: Check in after your introduction. See how the connection has unfolded and offer additional support if needed.

Being a bridge is more than just making introductions; it's about fostering relationships that can change lives. Your simple act of connecting others can lead to groundbreaking partnerships, innovative projects, and lifelong friendships.

Who can you introduce today that might create a ripple effect of positive change? Take the initiative and be the catalyst for someone's next big opportunity. The impact you make could be far-reaching and profoundly meaningful.

*

Again, I departed with an enriched sense of friendship and experience. Once more, leaving the African continent, I vowed to return soon. And so it was – more countries were on my list.

Visiting Africa wasn't just a convenient escape from New York winters to African summers. The true reason was much deeper. It intertwined with my work, as I often extended trips justified by speaking engagements to continue working, playing, and exploring in various locations. I thrive on a change of scenery, and Africa provided the perfect backdrop for both personal and professional growth, apart from adorning my life with its rich culture.

I travel to experience local life, not to sit in an all-inclusive hotel sipping cocktails. I once heard a high-ticket coach and influencer say she loved traveling because she could taste a different cocktail in each destination. Oh well, to each their own... For that, I could just stroll down the street in any big city, book a room, and visit the hotel bar each night. Or just any bar, if it's really about cocktails. No need to travel far for that!

Chapter 19
Mics, Meetings, and Magic: Spotlights and Soundwaves in Cameroon

Lessons in Spontaneity and Authenticity

In March 2018, along with my co-hosts Natalie from Cameroon/Italy and Monica from Georgia, we staged the *Cameroon Entrepreneurship Conference - Building Entrepreneurial Ecosystems in Africa* at the prestigious Hotel Mont Fébé in Yaoundé. It was an exhilarating first trip to Cameroon for me, made even more special as I'd long dreamed of visiting with my former Cameroonian love, a plan that never came to fruition.

The conference was a true passion project; we all poured our time and money into it without any monetary profit, but the rewards in gratitude, recognition, and human warmth were overwhelming. My topic was *Increase Your Impact to Be Seen in a Crowded Market*. Among the enthusiastic audience was a large group of students, eagerly soaking up our content. Meeting Sophie Ngassa and the other magnificent speakers we had engaged was another highlight, and we even enjoyed a big feature in the local newspaper, complete with color photos.

I also had the pleasure of doing a Calling the Women radio show with powerhouse Amy Banda from CRTV, whom I'd connected with years before this trip. We had an amazing time recording it at her studio and hanging out after. With Amy, I also spent chatting over several savory Cameroonian dinners at what became my favorite restaurant, Manuba – not just for their exquisite food and the lovely garden, but also for their music. The DJ even played some Haitian Kompa one night, in addition to Afrobeat and other African rhythms. Amy later also included me in an issue of Daybreak news.

The conference hosts were slated for a quick interview on a morning TV show with Pochi Tamba Nsoh, a renowned TV moderator with CRTV. For this, we had to rise at 4am to be at the studio early for make-up. As we sat waiting for our turn, we learned that only one of us would get airtime. This was quite disappointing after all our early-morning effort, especially since we had repeatedly announced our interview on social media. Fast forward...

After the conference, I decided to move to a small, simple hotel in a different part of the city, the Bellevue in the Mbankolo neighborhood. There were no phones in the guest rooms, and my cell phone service didn't work well in Yaoundé at all, let alone the GPS, which was completely nonfunctional. The wifi at the hotel was unreliable, and the only dependable phone was the landline at reception.

One of my last mornings in Yaoundé, the exuberant owner of the Bellevue came knocking on my door, excitedly shouting, "Hello, madam, I have CRTV station on the phone for you!" I dashed to the front desk to take the call. The voice on the other end informed me that I was expected at the studio by 11am to appear on the Midi Live show with Myra Nangeh, who had also MCed our conference, at noon. The Midi Live show is a bilingual program, catering to both English and French-speaking audiences. The caller, merely a messenger, had no further details to offer.

While thrilled about this surprise opportunity, coordinated by my friend Amy Banda, a few challenges arose. I had scheduled meetings for the day, and with no internet and unreliable cell phone service, contacting my meeting partners was tricky. Eventually, and in a frenzy, I managed to reschedule. The second challenge was finding a clean, TV-ready dress. With my trip nearing its end, I was running low on fancy outfits.

I opted for a colorful dress and a pair of matching heels that would do the job and hailed a taxi. The ride to the CRTV studios was chaotic, with traffic jams and several minor collisions, including a bump with a motorbike. No one seemed to care. The show must go on!

Despite the nerve-racking traffic, I arrived at the studio on time, where the make-up artist awaited me. I'm not usually a fan of heavy air conditioning, but this studio was sweltering. I waited in my seat, watching the beginning of the show until it was my turn.

The studio became the backdrop for a truly memorable exchange. Myra and I had a delightful, flowing conversation despite no content preparation. I had no idea what she would ask me. It was just one of those times when authenticity wins, and we ended up having a great conversation. A well-traveled chef in the background was cooking delicious Asian sesame chicken skewers, and a traditional Cameroonian band was opposite the couch we sat on. They had invited the band for me, knowing I loved dancing. This meant I had to get up and dance with them in my high skinny heels on a fluffy carpet! Despite never having danced to this rhythm before, it was incredibly fun. The band leader came up to teach me some moves, and Myra, an excellent dancer, joined in. It was all about having a great time and entertaining the audience, and we did just that!

My friends at CRTV later told me that viewers had written in to say they loved seeing me join in. Viewers praised the spontaneity, a testament to the power of embracing the unplanned and unexpected. They thought it was awesome, and so did I. It surely was a special moment, especially since it was entirely improvised on my end. And... being on a Cameroonian TV show – check!

Another opportunity that showed up for me while in Yaoundé was to speak at an event for about 50 women entrepreneurs set up by Santher Mbacham and her Imagenation team that we titled *Choreograph your success as a female leader in business & society*, aligned with my passion for dance. Other speakers were Leila Kigha and Gladys Viban, two tremendously powerful and inspiring Cameroonian speakers. At that event, I had the pleasure of meeting Njikta Ngwi, who later surprised me with a present: a beautifully embroidered Cameroonian shirt that she had designed herself.

I also was honored to be interviewed about my book, *Speak Up, Stand Out, and Shine*, at the hotel by Suzanne Belle Essengue from CRTV. She brought along a cameraman, and we enjoyed a fantastic conversation for her CRTV book show. Amy Banda came around as well, and we did a second show together, which this time was video-taped rather than just recording audio.

Thanks to Amy Banda's efforts, I subsequently appeared in magazines after interviews with Charles Tembei and Gilbert Ewehmeh, who featured me in their publications.

The host of the morning TV show, Pochi Tamba, once extended an invitation to her home for a sumptuous traditional lunch. Beyond the exquisite meal and conversation, we left with a treasured gift: a large piece of beautiful African fabric.

In return, I invited Pochi to lunch at one of my favorite restaurants. She graciously offered to show me around and took me to a quiet arts and crafts market where I picked up two beautiful necklaces. Later, I had the pleasure of dining with Pochi and her husband, Christopher, at a renowned chicken spot. Our dinner was a blend of business and pleasure, as we discussed Christopher's work at the University of Buea and other topics.

When Pochi temporarily relocated to New York to pursue film studies, she stayed with me until she settled into a permanent apartment. During her time in the city, we enjoyed a range of activities together, including a film documentary Pochi made of my Guinean fashion designer friend Mariame (who had a store down the street from my apartment), long walks in Central Park, and dance classes.

Back to my time in Yaoundé: I'm amazed at how many meetings I managed to fit into less than two weeks, despite the communication challenges posed by unreliable internet and phone service. Among these meetings was one with Prof. Willibroad Dze-Ngwa, Founding President of HEHIPEDS. He took me to a bustling area reminiscent of an Arabic bazaar, filled with shops and small food outlets.

Emilienne, a kind lady I had met through another organization, arranged a visit to the Minister of Women Empowerment and Family. I also explored several government ministries housed in neglected buildings; their ceilings festooned with dangling cables in urgent need of repair. She also took me to a street lined with tailor shops. She brought along some fabric and had a traditional Cameroonian dress made for me, which we collected just before my departure.

In Cameroon, my travel adventures sometimes involved hopping into collective cabs – essentially shared rides where you cram in with a mix of locals and never quite know where or when you'll get dropped off. With my lack of orientation in Yaoundé and the GPS of my U.S. phone not working due to a missing network, navigating this way was a real gamble. I'd often seek advice from people at bus stops to figure out what a fair fare would be, adding to the sense of unpredictability. My presence as a foreigner didn't go unnoticed; it was clear that I was a rare sight in these crowded taxis.

One morning, Pochi's husband Chistopher kindly picked me up from my hotel for a high-stakes meeting with some key business contacts. Our destination was a swanky part of the Palais des Congrès complex, where we were to enjoy breakfast at the chic restaurant. To avoid the notorious traffic, he opted for a shortcut through some smaller, unpaved streets.

It had rained heavily the night before, turning these shortcuts into a quagmire. One street was transformed into a bustling market – overflowing with vegetables, fruits, and people – all of it muddied by the previous night's rain. As we got stuck amid the chaos of vendors, bicycles, and an endless sea of people, it quickly became clear that we were at an impasse. Moving forward or backward was impossible.

Determined not to miss our meeting, Christopher enlisted the help of a young guy to guide us out. For a tip, of course. Navigating out of the jam was like threading a needle; every time we moved, people scrambled to avoid the car, and the mud splattered up to our windows. After a tense 20 minutes, we finally emerged onto clearer streets and made it to our meeting location. Remarkably, we arrived early – our contact was late, too!

At the same venue, I had the pleasure of meeting a fantastic group of women. Over the years, we've stayed in touch, and one of them even hosted a memorable "last supper" at her home with her family before driving me to the airport the night of my departure.

Leadership Wisdom – Key Takeaways

Unplanned Opportunities Often Make for Unforgettable Moments

As our TV show concluded, I couldn't help but marvel at the beauty of unplanned opportunities. These spontaneous moments, when embraced, often become the unforgettable highlights of our travels and lives.

Reflect on this: What would you have done if you had been in my shoes that morning at the Bellevue Hotel? Would you have stuck to your original plans out of convenience, or would you have seized the opportunity, even if it meant going out of your way to reschedule meetings? Be honest with yourself.

After reading my story, consider what you would do the next time such an opportunity presents itself in your life. Will you say yes and make it happen? Yes?

Authenticity Always Wins When Connecting with an Audience

I had no idea what to expect on the TV show. I'd never watched it, didn't know what questions the host would throw my way, and certainly hadn't anticipated being asked to dance – all on live TV in a country I'd just set foot in a few days earlier.

When I saw Myra, I was relieved. I hadn't even known she would be the show host. I decided to go with the flow, embracing whatever came my way. And that's exactly what I did. I took on the dance challenge without hesitation, and judging by the spectators' comments, the audience loved all of it.

This success boiled down to two things: I showed up authentically as myself, and I embraced the unexpected with a sense of adventure. I didn't spoil their fun surprise. It never occurred to me not to dance, despite the risk of looking foolish. I'm not a party pooper.

Think about a time when you turned down an offer or opportunity because you were afraid of making a fool of yourself. How often have you missed out on major fun and the chance to inspire others to take a risk and step into something new, even if it meant being imperfect?

Next time, can you find the courage to say yes? What's the real risk anyway? No one likes perfect people – they don't exist. They just might *look* perfect. (Except that as spiritual beings, we are *all* perfect as we are).

Dare to be you and dare to be real. The world needs more authenticity. So, the next time an unexpected opportunity comes your way, seize it. Show up as your true self, embrace the power of the moment, and inspire others to do the same.

*

When I left Cameroon, my bag was transformed. Instead of copies of my book I had sold and given away by the dozens, it was filled with gifts – a typical scenario when leaving the African continent. But my heart was even fuller, brimming with new friendships, dear memories, and rich experiences.

Little did I know, I was also bringing back an unexpected "gift," one that was far from welcome. More about that in the next chapter.

Chapter 20

A Sneaky Enemy Knocking Me Off My Feet... and Almost Out of Life

Lessons in Life, Death, and Self-Care

After arriving in an unusually cold spring in New York City, I quickly immersed myself in intense networking and prepared for a 3-day workshop in Qatar. An Indian company had hired me to deliver this training, and I was thrilled to teach the powerful content of my Powerful Leadership Transformation (PLT)™ framework, complemented by Conversational Intelligence (C-IQ)® tools, to a group of female leaders in Doha.

About two weeks after my return, I started feeling unwell. At first, I wasn't alarmed, but as my condition rapidly worsened and I felt extremely weak, I visited a CityMD urgent care walk-in in Harlem, not far from my home. After conducting some tests, they informed me that they had called an ambulance to take me to the hospital, as they suspected something serious. This is how I found myself in the emergency room of Mount Sinai Hospital, where it was determined that my blood pressure was dangerously low, and I was severely dehydrated. I stayed until I was reasonably rehydrated, and my blood pressure had normalized. At around 4:30am, they told me I had malaria. Despite this, I was released and sent home with a prescription for malaria medication. I rarely take medication, but I was advised that it was critical in this case. I debated whether to take it... I slowly walked home, slept until 11am (still feeling extremely weak and exhausted), and eventually walked over to the pharmacy to pick up my medication. Big mistake!

I took the prescribed dose, went back to bed as I still felt somewhat tired and weak, and just a few hours later, I felt so sick I could barely move. Desperate and unsure of what to do, I called 911 without even getting out of bed. About 30 minutes later, they picked me up in a wheelchair because I could no longer even walk. I literally had crawled to my apartment door so they wouldn't have to break it open. I was transported back to the same hospital, where I had to wait and prove I had insurance or could pay (typical US procedure!) before being admitted to the ICU. I could no longer eat, drink, or do anything by myself, let alone use a toilet. I was miserable, acutely aware that my life was hanging by a thread.

I felt so frail, I just let myself be treated like a puppet on a string... arm lifted, arm dropped, eyes barely open. This is usually not who I am at all! I'm someone who takes charge, who thrives on independence and strength. But in those moments, I was at the mercy of others, powerless and vulnerable, drifting in and out of consciousness. My body, once a vessel of determination, now felt like a fragile shell. The contrast was stark and unsettling, a haunting reminder of how quickly life can shift from control to chaos. And yet... at the same time, I felt this strange serenity. It was as if an ocean wave of peace was washing over me, soothing my apparent turmoil and bringing an unexpected calm. I felt like I was in the twilight zone; it was almost surreal.

The next day, when I was somewhat stabilized, I was transferred to a small, rather unappealing hospital room on a different floor, right next to the nurses' station. All I wanted to do was sleep, sleep, sleep. Unfortunately, it was noisy with the nurses chattering, my door left open most of the time, and one night, a man barged into my room looking for a relative, loudly complaining about something or other.

A large screen on the wall displayed serene natural sceneries on a continuous loop. Day in and day out, I watched these tranquil scenes, which oddly added to the mysterious sense of peace I still felt most of the time. This was the only thing I watched – no TV, no videos, no audios, no books. I felt mostly like sleeping and being passive, but with the constant noise in the hallway, I resigned myself to staring at the screen whenever I couldn't sleep.

Soon enough, my nagging memory kicked in: With the imminent trip to Qatar, I needed to alert the Indian company about my condition so they'd be prepared if I couldn't travel. After some back-and-forth messaging and realizing their reluctance to move the date, even for a week, I decided to tell them I'd be fine with the original dates, even though I still had to catch up on some preparation. I told myself I'd be fine, and I knew I would. However, the next day, they informed me they'd push the 4-day training back by a week.

Apart from the noise, the food was unbearable. I remembered the hospital food in Brazil – it wasn't gourmet, but it was light years ahead of this repulsive stuff. Ironically, patients received a huge menu titled "Your Nutrition Coach's Suggestions" (or something similar), filled with nicely sounding options, which turned out to be the most disgusting and unhealthy things I've ever seen (nutrition = zero!). If you weren't sick before, you surely would be after eating this, diabetes included! My first breakfast experience included a sugary, overly processed banana yogurt with all sorts of strange ingredients (I hate banana yogurt!), accompanied by a banana so brown it seemed picked from the compost (who'd serve a banana with a banana yogurt in the first place?), a tea bag, and some disgraceful mush I wouldn't want to taste in a lifetime! What I had picked was something along the lines of "fresh fruit, yogurt, and herbal tea." Even the tea was black instead of herbal.

For the following day, I chose only herbal tea and asked my friend Mimi to bring me croissants and fruit for breakfast – something edible – which she graciously did. Yet, during my entire stay, my request for herbal tea was ignored, and I ended up with black tea or water instead. They didn't even get that right. The whole situation would have been comical if it wasn't so ludicrous, given their pompous menu announcements. For lunch, I tried ordering fried fish with mashed potatoes, thinking it would be hard to mess up, and my appetite was picking up. The portion was huge (which I hadn't asked for), but the quality was indescribable.

The artificial rehydration had blown my body up like a balloon, so I wasn't really in the mood to eat much anyway. I was eagerly waiting to get back in shape to fit into my pants and in urgent need of more sleep if I wanted to recover in time for my trip. So, I asked to be released as soon as possible.

My Hungarian friend Ava, who lived all the way over in New Jersey, generously freed up time to pick me up in her car, take me food shopping, and then drop me off at home. By now feeling voracious from seeing fresh veggies and fruits again – finally, I made a huge pot of vegetable soup, ensuring I'd have something healthy and substantial for the next few days. I ended up making far more soup than I could ever eat.

Once the soup was ready, I ate my fill and then fell into bed, where I slept for a solid 15 hours!

When I emerged from my dreams, I was jolted into the stark reality of looming deadlines. I had to get my act together: finish the workshop content and slides, and urgently acquire a few more outfits. My existing dresses were all sleeveless, a fashion choice ill-suited for Qatar's dress code and the frigid air conditioning expected at the hotel.

Given my sluggish recovery, I had to tread carefully. Even a brisk walk in the now warm spring air could potentially send me back to the hospital. My body was still in recovery mode and pushing it too hard was not an option. With every little physical effort, my heart pounded like a drum, a stark reminder of just how delicate my condition remained.

A few remote holistic sessions with my BodyTalk instructor Terryann from Canada, combined with immune-boosting remedies like artemisia, accelerated my recovery over the next few days. Thanks to these interventions, I was able to complete everything and wrap up my preparations just in time.

Leadership Wisdom – Key Takeaways

Your Health Deserves Top Priority

When your life hangs by a thread, you have two choices: prioritize your health or risk everything. A serious health scare not only highlights life's fragility but also underscores the critical importance of self-care.

Self-care is not a luxury; it's a fundamental part of self-leadership, and your health and well-being should always come first.

Consider this: How often do you prioritize your health and well-being?

- Do you set aside time to work out and stay fit?
- Are you getting enough physical activity?
- Do you allow yourself adequate rest?
- Do you have a routine that helps you recharge?
- Are you getting sufficient alone time?
- How do you start your day?
- Are you eating nutritious foods and staying hydrated?
- What are your stress levels like?
- Do you know how to manage excessive stress?
- Do you respect your physical and mental needs?
- Would a weekly massage or reflexology enhance your well-being?

Reflect on these questions honestly and adjust your habits as needed. Your future self will thank you!

*

As I sank into my seat on the plane to Qatar, I felt grateful for the opportunity to rest during the flight and eagerly anticipated meeting the training participants.

Chapter 21
Teaching Under Doha's Sun

Lessons in Business Transactions

Stepping off the plane in Doha, I was immediately hit by the hot, dry air, intensifying my already unquenchable thirst. My body was still healing, craving hydration, but as long as I moved slowly, I managed. After a taxi dropped me off at the hotel, the whirlwind of preparation meetings began, with the 3-day workshop kicking off the next morning.

I was introduced to a diverse group of eight women, all leaders within the same oil industry organization, ranging from newcomers to seasoned professionals. We had arranged to include my book as part of the workshop materials. Though my contract specified that I couldn't directly sign up any of the participants for one-on-one coaching, the book, with my contact details inside, provided a direct way for them to reach out. And sure enough, on one of the workshop days, one of the more experienced participants approached me, expressing interest in hiring me as her coach. I reminded her of the need to go through the agency, which led to a follow-up email exchange. That evening, during a meeting with the agency rep, I informed him of the interaction. He thanked me for my transparency, assuring me we'd work out the details together.

Imagine my shock, then, when, after a brief rest, I opened my email to find a message from the same agency rep accusing me of breaching our agreement by speaking with the participant. Was I supposed to ignore her completely and turn her away?

Of course, this was just an excuse to dock 30% of my pay. The agency claimed they lost two or three participants due to the date change, which affected their profit since the fee was per participant. Remember, it was *their* decision to move the date, not mine. This was their way of clawing back some money – by taking it from me. They knew full well that enforcing the contract or pursuing legal action was impractical due to the costs involved. So, they took advantage of the situation. Yet another lesson learned, this time in business: Never provide the full extent of a service before being paid in full, unless you're prepared to risk losing part of your compensation. I know this may sometimes be challenging. In any case, get as much as you can in advance or in increments as you fulfill the agreement, depending on the scope of the project.

While this episode cast a shadow over my time in Doha, the overall rewards outweighed the loss. For instance, one participant who was too shy to introduce herself on the first day surprised us all by confidently volunteering for an assignment in front of the room on the third day. Totally made my heart sing!

After several days of intense training, dining, and bonding with the remarkable group of women, one of them sent a generous gift of local delicacies to my room as a heartfelt "thank you." With the workshop concluded, I was looking forward to spending an extra day exploring Doha and its surroundings.

On the evening following the final training session, I took a cab to the renowned Souq Waqif and wandered through the vibrant bazaar. The next day, I visited the Museum of Islamic Art and strolled along the picturesque harbor. Despite generally enjoying the heat, my still-recovering body felt weighed down by the oppressive warmth. As I walked outside the museum, I stumbled and injured my knee. Though it hurt and left me limping, I brushed it off. And yet, it was a stark reminder of how precious good health truly is.

Undeterred, I continued to explore the Corniche (the harbor promenade) and ventured out to the more remote Pearl and Katara Cultural Village. Finding a cab back proved challenging, but a kind man in a parking lot agreed to drive me for a few Qatari riyals. I was profoundly grateful, as I was running out of steam (and low on water).

I typically would have extended my stay to visit the desert dunes, but given my health, I opted to return to New York the following day.

The flight home proved more arduous than expected. A generous layover in London turned into a race against time when our flight landed at Heathrow Airport about 90 minutes late. We circled endlessly before finally touching down, and the bus to my connecting terminal took another 30 minutes to arrive. I found myself sprinting down what felt like an interminable corridor, passing countless gates, heart racing and feeling faint. Despite my delicate state, I was determined to make my connection, hoping my heart would not fail me. I arrived at the gate just two minutes before it closed, a testament to my stubborn resolve, but also completely exhausted.

Leadership Wisdom – Key Takeaways

Securing Payment in Advance: A Key Strategy for International Transactions

After my experience with the Indian agents, I decided to request advance payment when approached by a London-based agency. When they refused, I opted not to work with them. The payment wasn't substantial enough anyway, and while the teaching assignment per se seemed interesting, nothing justified the risks without pre-payment. I wasn't willing to endure another potentially problematic situation.

When engaging in international transactions with unfamiliar parties, it's prudent to secure payment in advance to mitigate risks and protect your interests, at least as soon as you arrive at the site of fulfillment. The inherent uncertainty of working with individuals or entities from different countries can expose you to various financial risks, including delayed payments or non-payment. By requiring payment upfront, you ensure that your work or goods are compensated for before they are delivered. This approach not only safeguards your financial stability but also fosters a sense of security in the transaction, helping to establish a more professional and trustworthy business relationship. In an international context, where communication and legal recourse may be more complex (and the latter costly), upfront payment serves as a crucial risk management strategy.

*

As my flight from Doha to New York soared through the night sky, my mind was already racing ahead to future adventures. Africa was on my mind. I had forged promising connections online, and the anticipation of what these might lead to was intoxicating. The unknowns ahead promised excitement and perhaps a touch of unexpected events – my thoughts buzzed with potential stories yet to unfold, and when I fell asleep in my seat, these new adventures already came to life in my dreams.

Chapter 22

Leadership and Local Flavor: Immersing Myself in Uganda's Heartbeat

Lessons in Kindness and Seizing Opportunities to Inspire

2019 was a whirlwind of travel for me. In June, Nigerian Ken Giami invited me to Atlanta, Georgia, as a panelist for the USAfrica business conference. Following the event, we agreed that I would lead a 2-day Women's Leadership Development Masterclass at the EU-African Summit in Stockholm, Sweden, organized by the Centre for Economic and Leadership Development (CELD). The masterclass was designed for Nigerian women, and on the third day, I also spoke on a panel when the event expanded to include a broader audience, bringing in local women of African descent.

The experience was incredibly rewarding. We had such a wonderful time together, and of course, there was dancing – what would a women's leadership class be without it? I fondly remember being asked to take photos with every single participant, and I so love those pics!

One of the women, Finney, who has held several government-related and women-centered roles in Gombe State, later reached out to hire me as the keynote speaker and trainer for an event in Abuja, Nigeria, where I would have been responsible for most of the content. Just as we signed the contract in early 2020, the world turned upside down with travel restrictions and lockdowns, derailing our plans. Finney tried to relocate the event to the UAE, but similar challenges prevented it from happening.

I was also deep in discussions with Bashirat, another summit speaker and Group Executive at FBN Lagos, about an exciting training collaboration, but unfortunately, the events of 2020 brought those plans to a halt as well. These two projects would have undoubtedly been among my favorites…

In August 2019, I decided to give up my apartment, as I had an extensive itinerary ahead – five months on the road and in the air. First, I was set to fly to Phoenix, AZ, to present at a SHRM conference. From there, I planned to spend a month in Johannesburg, where I was slated to speak at a conference as well as a smaller event for entrepreneurs. After a quick stop in New York City to repack, I headed to Maryland to teach several sessions at a firm's event in Cambridge. Following that, I'd penciled in a visit home to see my family in Germany. Next, I was scheduled to speak at a conference in New York City, and then I had planned to travel to Uganda and Rwanda for two months.

It was a tough decision to leave my apartment. I loved its location on the northwestern corner of Central Park, directly across from the park entrance and right next to the subway station, which was literally just outside our building door… and my landlord Franc, who'd been extremely collaborative, helping me rent the place out and save on rent at times while I was gone for several weeks. I had kept my rental agreements flexible on purpose, living in furnished apartments after moving from Brazil and leaving all my furniture and many other belongings behind. I wanted the freedom to move easily. With five months of travel ahead and New York City rents, it made sense to let even this apartment go, put my things in a small storage unit, and find a new place when I returned.

Looking back, my intuition was protecting me, sensing what was to come in early 2020. But that's skipping ahead...

At the beginning of December, I boarded a plane to Kampala. I had previously connected with Abdul Nassar Mukasa from the Institute of Advanced Leadership Uganda, located in the Nsambya neighborhood of Kampala, and we had agreed to explore the possibility of long-term collaboration, starting with a smaller project on the ground. Nassar and his colleague Grace, who graciously (pun intended) opened her home to me during my stay, picked me up at the airport. At Grace's house in the Diplomatic Zone Makindye, I was warmly greeted by her daughters, two granddaughters. There was also a fierce guard dog who kept the property secure and was so fearsome that I never even saw him.

Unlike my other travels, I was driven around by locals most of the time. Each morning, we enjoyed coffee at Grace's home, which had a subtle ginger flavor that took me a moment to appreciate. By the second day, I found myself loving the combination, along with the homemade chapatis and a variety of fresh fruits. Uganda's climate is perfect for growing an abundance of fruits, and matoke (a type of green banana or plantain) is a staple you can find almost everywhere. The Ugandan tradition of cooking a big meal at least once a day meant that Grace's household had a cook, as she was often busy at the office. We usually ordered lunch in at the office, with portions that were always more than I could handle, and we had dinner at home.

The house itself was spacious, with two floors, but had an unusual feature: no internal doors, only curtains, except for one door to a large office. This took some getting used to, but as a seasoned traveler, adaptability is key. Since hot water for showers had to be boiled in the kitchen, the ladies would bring a bucket of it up to the bathroom on the second floor for me every morning, insisting on doing so despite my protests. Their generosity and hospitality were boundless, and it made me feel truly cared for.

In gratitude for Grace's hospitality, I offered her some holistic treatments, which she greatly appreciated, especially as she was dealing with a health condition at the time. It was my way of giving back to this kind and generous host, in addition to contributing groceries, of course.

Sylvia, another colleague we shared our office with, was also a person whose generosity knew no bounds. One day, Sylvia picked me up for lunch at a community house near her home. The meal was prepared by a group of several women from the Salaama Perfect Women's Community in Makindye Division, including herself and her daughter. It was a wonderful experience, sharing a meal cooked with care and enjoying the warm company of these amazing women. I'll never forget that delicious fish!

The Institute of Advanced Leadership, under Nassar's and guidance, organized an enriching full-day training event for the leaders of the Uganda Scouts Association at their offices, where I had the opportunity to lead a session. Despite the short notice, the day proved to be both productive and engaging, culminating in a delightful lunch with the attendees.

I was also honored to take part in a special event at the Institute, which blended a meeting, celebration, and Q&A session with the students. One of the highlights for me was fielding their questions and exchanging perspectives, which was incredibly rewarding.

Additionally, thanks to Sylivia's exceptional coordination, I had the privilege of visiting the Bulange in Kampala – the heart of the Administration and Parliament of the Kingdom of Buganda. There, I met with representatives from the Nabagereka Development Foundation (the Buganda Kingdom Queen Mother's Foundation) and their staff, as well as other prominent Ugandan figures, all of who eagerly posed for photos with us, adding a personal touch to the visit.

One day, Sylivia arrived at Grace's place with her two children, Susan and Ricky. Together, we set off for Nampunge situated outside of Kampala/north-west of Kampala, where we were to visit a rural community of coffee farmers: Gala Nampunge Multi-purpose Co-operative Society. This community is known for its exceptional coffee products as well as craftsmanship, producing a wide range of items, from baskets to coffee and rugs. On the way, we picked up fruit tree seedlings, which we planted at a newly built property. I've since heard that those trees have flourished, yielding an abundant harvest of mangos and other fruits.

Upon arrival at the community center, we were warmly welcomed by Jesica from the management team, and a large group of locals. They didn't only introduce me to the place and explain everything in detail; they also showered me with more gifts than I could possibly take back to the U.S., so I left the larger ones with my hosts. Before we left, we took a group photo with everyone, capturing the warm spirit of the day.

On the way back, we stopped at a roadside stand for chicken skewers, where vendors walked up and down selling street food. In a humorous twist, I received a marriage proposal through the car window from the man selling us the skewers – it must have been love at first sight, haha.

At one point, I had the opportunity to be interviewed by Rest TV Uganda, where they aired an episode about the Institute. We also met with various other leaders and visited a hotel for a potential future joint venture event. Through these interactions and other connections I made, I forged several valuable relationships, including one with Sandie, the CEO of a bee products business.

Throughout our time together, the Advanced Leadership Institute team and I were diligently crafting a Memorandum of Understanding (MOU) to formalize a long-term collaboration set to kick off in 2020. We envisioned a promising partnership, but fate had other plans. Little did we know that our ambitious goals would soon be dashed, at least for the immediate future, as travel restrictions were imposed.

And, naturally, no visit would be complete without dance! Knowing my passion for it, Nassar and his friends took me to an open-air Bwola dance performance one evening. I was also invited to another social gathering featuring a local band and dancer another night. True to form, the dancer pulled me into the center of the circle, where I had the chance to join in the dance for a thrilling minute or two. I think I didn't do too badly, considering it was my first time... On the African continent, you could literally learn a new dance every day of the year!

On the day of my departure, I was warmly invited to lunch at Nassar's home in Kabalagala Parish, Village Muzaana zone. His wife had prepared a delicious meal, and their children presented me with beautifully wrapped gifts, using newspaper for a creative touch. After the meal, Nassar gave me a tour of his neighborhood before he and his friend Hassan, another generous soul and knowledgeable tour guide operator for Uganda and Kenya, drove me to the airport. As we slowly moved through the bustling, narrow streets, the car was filled with the sounds of music from people's radios and the rich aromas of various street foods wafting in through the windows.

Once again, I left with gifts in my bag, including a dress specially made for me, but the most precious takeaway was the treasure trove of beautiful memories – of warm hospitality, planting trees, savoring delicious fish, and forming lasting friendships.

Leadership Wisdom – Key Takeaways

Kindness Goes a Long Way

During my stay in Kampala, I experienced a profound lesson in the power of generosity and connection. Each day, I was surrounded by individuals whose acts of kindness were not just gestures, but powerful inspirations that shaped my journey. From Nassar's thoughtful help to Grace's and Sylivia's warm hospitality to my interactions with students, Scout leaders, cooperatives, entrepreneurs, and everyone else I had a chance to meet, every encounter was a reminder of the incredible impact one can have on others through simple acts of support and encouragement.

Seize Every Opportunity to Inspire Greatness in Others

In every moment, there lies an opportunity to inspire. Whether it's through a small act of kindness, a supportive gesture, or sharing a bit of your expertise, you have the power to make a difference. Embrace these chances with open arms. Your actions, no matter how seemingly insignificant, can create ripples of positivity and change.

Remember, inspiring others often starts with recognizing and seizing the moments that come your way. Nothing is random. So, grab every opportunity to inspire, and watch as the world transforms around you.

As a leader, you have countless opportunities to practice kindness in ways that can deeply impact your team. Here are three specific ways to start:

- Show genuine appreciation: Make it a habit to acknowledge the efforts of your team members, whether through a simple "thank you," a handwritten note, or public recognition during meetings. This small act can significantly strengthen morale and foster a sense of belonging.
- Offer your time and support: When a team member is struggling, take the time to listen and offer your help. A gesture of support can make a world of difference.
- Show that you care about your team's growth and development: Be not just a leader, but also a coach to them. If you're too busy or feel this isn't your strongest skill, consider hiring a coach to support you. This could involve helping you develop and integrate coaching into your leadership style or working directly with your team. In return, your team will likely demonstrate greater loyalty and dedication.

Remember, inspiring others often starts with recognizing and seizing the moments that come your way. Nothing is random. So, grab every opportunity to inspire through kindness, and watch as the world transforms around you.

*

On the brief flight from Kampala to Kigali, I found myself reflecting on the remarkable generosity of my hosts and the Institute's team. Nassar had even gone out of his way to drive me to a shopping mall to purchase a reliable internet modem. I needed it for recording an online TV show, as the local connection was too unstable. Thanks to this device, the broadcast went off without a hitch. Nassar also ensured the office stayed open for me to guest on the show late in the evening, and IT support was available.

Grace had opened her home to me, and Sylivia's impeccable coordination and chauffeuring took us to numerous destinations. Hassan's drive to the airport was another gesture of kindness. Their hospitality was truly boundless.

Chapter 23
Kigali Unscripted: Workshops and Unexpected Encounters

Lessons in Passion Projects and Meaningful Connections While Traveling

Kigali – what a stark contrast to Kampala! Though geographically close, the two cities are worlds apart in many respects. This makes traveling so exciting: Discovering our differences on the one hand, and the commonalities that unite us, on the other.

One of the most striking features of hilly Kigali is its impeccably clean streets. Cleanliness is taken seriously here; plastic bags are banned and eating in the streets is considered improper.

My first few nights were spent at Select Hotel, a charming boutique establishment owned by Thérèse, whom I met through my friend Bisila from New York. Thérèse welcomed me warmly, and we enjoyed delightful dinners (great chef!) on the garden terrace of her hotel. One evening, we were joined by Boita, Bisila's brother, who was in Rwanda for a business project. Boita and I quickly became good friends and had many engaging conversations about our businesses, and about life in Spain, Bali, and Equatorian Guinee.

I was thrilled when Thérèse introduced me to a traditional Gusaba – a Rwandan wedding tradition where the groom's family formally requests the bride. Although I didn't understand Kinyarwanda, I was captivated by the expressive "battle" of wits and pranks, much like the theater performance I once attended in Bangkok where the story was conveyed through expressions to me rather than words. The Gusaba ceremony was held on a hot day under a large white tent, with dancers performing the traditional Rwandan Intore and Amaraba dances to the rhythm of live drums. It was my first encounter with Rwandan dance, and I was mesmerized by the elegance and grace of both the men and women. I couldn't believe this beautiful tradition had eluded me for so long.

On the weekend, Thérèse took me to a friend's mansion in a rural area, where we enjoyed a sumptuous Rwandan meal with a large group of friends. Another day, she invited me to her family's house in the city, which featured a huge oval balcony, and we had a lovely buffet dinner there with a group of her friends. Staying at her hotel truly felt like being with family.

The main reason for my trip to Kigali was to conduct training for a project led by Grace, a driven social entrepreneur I met at a summit in Ghana. Grace had invited me to teach a five-day workshop to her team of ten at the University of Kigali campus, where they had an office. The campus is vast, and on my first day, I struggled to find Grace because I hadn't instructed the cab driver to drop me at the correct entrance. When we finally met, we greeted each other with a warm hug, overjoyed to reconnect.

Grace introduced me to her enthusiastic team. Using my Powerful Leadership Transformation (PLT)™ framework as a guide, I led them through a week of intensive training, sharing insights and strategies for success in both their personal and professional lives. The framework was complemented by a day of communication and public speaking teachings.

Together, we crafted a new team vision, a collaborative effort that took an entire afternoon. We wanted to ensure everyone's input was valued and that the entire team was committed to executing this shared vision. I also vividly remember their keen interest in the topic of a "Self-Empowering Mindset." The work we did was so impactful that they manifested a significant amount of funding for their project, or at least accelerated its approval. The exciting news arrived during a phone call while we were at a photo studio, waiting for a group shot they had organized.

The university campus was complete with a canteen, where we enjoyed our lunches together. Every day, we served ourselves generously from the buffet, replenishing the energy spent during our all-day sessions. Lunchtime was a chance to relax and share personal stories, further strengthening our bonds.

At the end of each day, some of us would exchange a few dance moves to loosen up, shake off the day's intensity, and integrate our learnings. This playful tradition led to a memorable night of Afrobeat dancing at a small museum with an outdoor dance floor and DJ. We showcased our best moves and had an amazing time, fostering a beautiful sense of connection and camaraderie. After our dance night, I took a motorbike taxi home, feeling grateful for the rich experiences and new friendships.

Except for my morning trips to the campus and trips with baggage, for which I'd take a regular cab, I usually opted for motorbike taxis. The drivers always carried an extra helmet for their passengers. These rides were typically around a dollar or less. Although the motorbike riders did not speak English or French, I managed to negotiate fares and explain my destinations using hand gestures and landmarks. Having local friends nearby made it easier to communicate, but I always found a way to manage on my own when necessary, which was most of the time, like when heading out for meetings or for the night… After asking around, I found a couple of spots to get some Kizomba, Semba, Salsa, and even Kompa dancing under my belt.

In exchange for the training, I was provided with a 10-night stay at a small Airbnb studio in the Kicukiro neighborhood, owned by Mariam and Santiago. Moving from the hotel to the Airbnb on an extremely hot day, Grace, Bexy, and I arrived at the gate only to find the owners were not home. We waited for about an hour, sitting on my suitcase outside the property until they finally arrived. Once settled, everything went smoothly. There was a grocery store a 10-minute walk away, and I found everything I needed within a reasonable walking distance.

Another unforgettable encounter – actually, several – was with Raoul Rugamba, a dynamic local entrepreneur. Raoul later invited me to return in late March 2020 to speak at a major event he was organizing at the Kigali Convention Center – one of many gigs on my calendar canceled that year for… well, you know why. However, we continue to keep in touch through occasional virtual exchanges.

One day, Raoul generously took on the role of my guide, driving me around Kigali and showing me the city's vibrant culture. We had lunch at one of his favorite restaurants, followed by drinks at a trendy outdoor nightlife spot later that day, where we met one of his entrepreneurial friends. The energy and innovation I witnessed in these two men were inspiring.

Raoul is also one of my links to writer and motivational speaker Immaculée Ilibagiza (perhaps you've heard of her). She invited me to dinner at her home, where she shared her incredible story over a delicious Rwandan meal with her friends and family. It was a night of profound conversation and connection.

Through Raoul's intervention, I also had notable exchanges with Agnès, the Executive Director at the Rwanda Chamber of Women Entrepreneurs, and Mireille from Kora Coaching Group. Plus, young entrepreneurs seemed to find their way to me from all sides. Each introduction added to the depth of my experiences and insights during my time in Kigali.

As December 31st approached, I was planning to attend Congolese singer Fally Ipupa's New Year's Eve show, but it was canceled, likely for political reasons. Instead, Mariam and Santiago invited me to join them for dinner with a group of friends, followed by fireworks near the Convention Center. We had a wonderful time, and I met Nastassja from South Africa, who became a friend and occasional dinner guest at my later Airbnb; I had to move as this place wasn't available for my entire 1-month stay.

And so it was that after the ten days, I moved to a spacious Airbnb in the Rukiri 1 area, hosted by Ishimwe, a true super host. The location was near a busy road, making it easy to catch a motorbike taxi. One day, however, two riders stopped and began fighting over who would take me. With them being unable to reach an agreement, I decided to go back inside and leave them to their dispute. My downstairs Airbnb neighbor Pierre, a Rwandan living in South Korea, saw me return and offered to help. Grateful for his assistance, I accepted, as the riders were still arguing, and I needed to get to my meeting. Eventually, I was able to depart with one of the riders, hoping the other wouldn't follow us and pick another fight, which thankfully didn't happen.

When I returned early that evening, my neighbor's place was already in full swing. He was about to head back to South Korea, and his friends had gathered for a farewell party. As I walked through the gate into our front yard, I was greeted with warm laughter and immediately handed a beer. I figured I'd stay for a drink, but once I stepped into the large living room, I saw about ten young men, one of whom was stirring a huge pot of soup. With music playing, the guys asking me to dance (you know it's my thing), and everyone in such high spirits, leaving after just one drink didn't seem like an option.

As the night went on, more people arrived – girlfriends, sisters, and friends – turning the gathering into a full-blown party. I ended up staying much longer than I'd planned, caught up in the fun. But with a tour to Akagera National Park booked for the next morning and a pickup scheduled for 5am sharp, I knew I couldn't stay too late. Despite the fun and great conversations, I eventually tore myself away, although the music kept me awake for another hour or two.

The next morning, we set out before sunrise. The drive to the park was an experience in itself. As soon as we reached the outskirts of the city, the landscape changed: people carrying staggering amounts of produce on their heads or shoulders; or pushing carts and bikes with huge baskets loaded to the brim with goods, from vegetables to large canisters of liquid. It was a colorful, seemingly endless parade on either side of the road, all under the dim light of dawn. These were farmers and workers, bringing their goods from rural areas to the markets. I couldn't help but admire their extraordinary resilience, even though to them, it was likely just another part of their daily routine – one without the convenience of motor vehicles, with even their bikes serving more as carts than as something they could ride. I will never forget the images of these caravans on either side of the road...

On our way to the park, we stopped in a village to grab some water and snacks. Once we arrived, we met our guide and swapped the driver's car for a jeep. The day was overcast, with a light drizzle, and the park's paths were sludgy and at certain places thick with knee-high mud that seemed almost impossible to traverse. But thanks to our skilled driver and the jeep's four-wheel drive, we managed to push through.

As we ventured deeper into the park, we encountered large families of playful baboons and a variety of other wildlife, including enormous hippopotamuses, elegant giraffes, and... finally... an elephant! I'd told my two companions that finding an elephant was at the top of my list – I've always had a special predilection for them. We kept driving, winding through the forested areas, and then suddenly, an elephant appeared on the path ahead of us. It was about 150-200 feet away (forgive me, I'm not the best at estimating distances), but even though elephants aren't as fast as hippos, they can certainly charge – and they're massive!

The elephant started moving toward our car, and the guide, who knew elephants well, immediately told us that this one was not happy, even before the elephant started charging. The driver reacted quickly, shifting into reverse. But with the muddy roads, our progress was slow, even with his expert handling. The elephant kept getting closer and closer, until it spotted a narrow path off to its right that led into the forest. Thankfully and unexpectedly, it chose to disappear into the woods, opting for "flight" rather than "fight" – a huge relief!

Just imagine if there had been another vehicle behind us... we wouldn't have been able to reverse quickly enough! After a few minutes to catch our breath and recover from the shock, we continued on our way. That's when we discovered the source of the elephant's distress: a car had approached it too closely from the opposite direction. Feeling trapped between two vehicles, it had understandably panicked.

The rest of our safari was less adventurous but no less thrilling. As we made our way back to the city, the guide rode with us until we reached his village, giving him and the driver a chance to chat while I relaxed in the back seat. It was the perfect way to wrap up my visit to Rwanda.

And so eventually, with a heart full of sweet memories and promising new plans, I departed. Unfortunately, those plans quickly vaporized – after all, it was 2020!

Leadership Wisdom – Key Takeaways

Passion Projects: The True Value Beyond Money

In the end, passion projects often offer rewards that transcend financial compensation. During my 5-day workshop in Kigali, my accommodation was covered in exchange for my expertise, rather than a traditional fee. This arrangement not only provided a unique opportunity to immerse myself in a different culture but also allowed me to forge valuable connections and impact lives in meaningful ways. The real payoff came from the experience, the relationships built, and the satisfaction of contributing to something meaningful. Passion projects, while they may not always line your pockets, can enrich your life in unexpected and profoundly rewarding ways.

What's a passion project you've been dreaming of but keep postponing? Imagine taking the first step towards making it a reality. What if you started today?

Extend Your Travel: Discover More with a Longer Stay

When you can, extend your short-term travel for a deeper experience. A longer stay lets you fully immerse yourself in the local culture, build stronger connections, and gain a more comprehensive understanding of your destination. For example, lengthening my visit to Kigali beyond the week of the workshop allowed me to engage more meaningfully with the community and experience the city beyond its surface, in ways a brief trip wouldn't allow for. By taking the time to stay longer, you turn a fleeting visit into a richer, more profound exposure to local life.

Most of us are busy people, and that often leads us to skim the surface, not just during our travels but also in our daily interactions. This tendency can extend to our conversations, relationships, and even our approach to leadership. When we're pressed for time, it's easy to settle for superficial exchanges and miss out on the deeper, more meaningful connections that lie beneath.

Imagine the possibilities if you took the time to engage in deeper conversations with your team. What insights, ideas, or hidden strengths might emerge if you fostered a more profound dialogue? By extending your efforts to understand and connect on a deeper level, you could uncover valuable perspectives and build stronger, more cohesive relationships that drive both personal and professional growth.

*

As I boarded the plane back home, my heart full of memories and my mind buzzing with possibilities, I knew that this journey had changed me in ways I could never have imagined. For in embracing the unknown and stepping outside of my comfort zone, I had discovered a new sense of purpose and a renewed appreciation for the beauty and rich diversity of the world we live in.

Chapter 24
Four Years as a Quasi-Nomad

Lessons in Freedom, Safety, and Power

By the end of January, back in New York, I was already planning my return to Kigali for late March, with more travels to follow. I decided to arrange temporary housing for now, with the intention of finding something more permanent later in the year. However, things took an unexpected turn, and all my travel plans changed.

From March 2020 to April 2024, this ended up being my trajectory (I'll try to get the sequence right): Playa del Carmen, Long Island, Jersey City, Weehawken, New York City, Munich, Miami Beach, Colorado, El Paso, Merritt Island, Miami, Tulum, Miami Beach, Phoenix, Chicago, Munich, Paris, Munich, Zanzibar Town, Miami Beach, Lyon, Munich, Lyon, Miami, Lyon, New York, to eventually split myself up between Miami, New York, and Lyon.

Why, you ask? – I'm glad you asked. Let me explain:

In mid-March 2020, I celebrated my birthday with my friend Peju, making the best of a chilly day filled with relentless rain and storms – not exactly the kind of weather I'd hoped for. But we didn't let that dampen our spirits and made the best of it! With complimentary tickets to Art on Paper, an annual arts fair, we started the day surrounded by creativity, taking photos with the most original pieces. Afterward, we headed to Vapiano, one of my favorite spots for fast, healthy Italian food in a warm, communal setting – one of many places that, sadly, disappeared soon after. But back to my birthday! We savored their amazing tomato soup crowned with fresh basil leaves and paired with a glass (or two) of Italian white wine, before making our way to LunÀtico, a cozy Brooklyn bar where the legendary Nkumu Katalay was performing with his band that night. I was in for a treat! Having this concert happen on my birthday felt like divine timing, and it was the perfect ending to a rainy day.

The next day, the sun finally came out, and my favorite friend and Kompa dancer, Chris, drove in from Long Island so we could enjoy lunch at the Lido in Harlem. Little did I know, it would be the last time I'd see him for three and a half years! The following Monday, I was supposed to speak at Lloyds, but – predictably – the event was canceled, marking the beginning of a cascade of cancellations: gigs in Kigali, Nairobi, Kampala, Johannesburg, London, Abuja, Kansas City, Honolulu, goodbye!

On March 10, I made my way to Katra on Bowery Street, one of my favorite spots for Kompa and Kizomba at the time. As I descended the stairs to the Kizomba party, I was met with an almost deserted basement and a sparse crowd of just ten people scattered around. The energy never picked up, so after an hour, I decided to leave. Later that week, I went to a networking event at a WeWork in Midtown, which usually would draw a large crowd. This time, however, only about ten networkers showed up.

With the lockdown looming over the City of New York like an invisible, but palpable gray blanket, I decided to escape the nightmare around me. All my dance classes and events had vanished from one moment to the next, with studios and bars following the mandates.

It was too depressing to see what was going on around me and how easily entire populations were controlled with fear and illogical prohibitions and rules without questioning them. Even though I didn't fully grasp what was happening – despite being relatively well-informed and aware, also thanks to my friend Susan (call it "awake" if you will, though the following year clearly added a whole new dimension to it) – I must admit I was caught off guard... What was crystal clear, however, was that something was seriously wrong, and I needed to figure it out.

I certainly didn't want to be imprisoned in a big city that's supposed to never sleep but now had all its lights off – too eerie! I felt like a lonely traveler in a metropolis of 19 million people, a solitary soul searching for the meaning of this situation. The "city that never sleeps" had morphed into a ghost town, stripped of its liveliness and echoing scenes from a horror movie I'd watched in my teens. It was overwhelming! This was just too much! As a freedom-lover, I thought to myself, "I'm outta here!"

At the time, I was living in a charming, furnished one-bedroom apartment on 145th Street in Harlem, a place I truly loved. With a week still left on my short-term lease, I didn't want to risk border restrictions tightening up. So, I packed up all my belongings, stuffed them into my storage unit, grabbed a bag of summer clothes and my laptop, and headed off to Playa del Carmen, Mexico, which welcomed me with open arms.

In Playa, I shared an apartment next to a golf course with an Airbnb host from a previous visit, Sandy. It was a win-win as it was a tough time for tourism. So, I was already familiar with the area and the premises, which included a swimming pool. In the meantime, Sandy had adopted a little dog named Suerte (which means "luck"). Because of her occasional wickedness and her predilection for nibbling our toes and making a mess with the soil in the plant pots, I affectionately nicknamed her Mala Suerte ("bad luck").

We often strolled around the golf course with Suerte, and I'd frequently see signs warning about alligators, said to have a particular appetite for attacking puppies. One day, I suggested we try a different route that I had discovered during a previous visit. Sandy agreed, and we set off along this new path instead of our usual loop. As we rounded a cluster of palm trees and bushes that obscured the view of one of the ponds, I felt a sudden, unsettling premonition. Just five seconds later, as we emerged from behind the palm trees, there it was: an alligator out of the water, only about 60 feet away! Sandy quickly scooped up Suerte (we certainly didn't want any *mala suerte* befalling her or us) and we continued on our way. Thankfully, the alligator soon retreated into the water, leaving only its large, watchful eyes sticking out.

One day, as I walked over to the beach, which was about 30 minutes away, I saw that access to the ocean was prohibited, I approached one of the security guards to ask her why that was. Why would people not be allowed to swim in the sea? She said it was because there were too many dead bodies floating down from the U.S. because of covid, hence there was a risk of intoxication. She said this with such a straight face that I wasn't sure whether she was serious or joking… although it could really only be a joke!

Apart from long walks and occasional bike rides, I spent most of my time at the apartment, focusing on adapting to the new reality by seeking out virtual speaking engagements and online networking opportunities. The abrupt halt of in-person events was a major setback, especially after the considerable effort I had put into lining up a busy 2024 speaking schedule. To make up for it, I explored every possible avenue online. Denise Rodaro, who frequently invited me to present on Argentine TV channels (iredes.net, LTV, RegiónNet), provided a valuable opportunity to work in Spanish once more. I vividly remember literally sweating through one of them when the air conditioning in our apartment went out on a particularly humid day.

About a year earlier, I had started a Roundtable with a group of ten leaders from the Finance and Legal sectors. These gatherings were initially held in person at their firms, which generously sponsored us with breakfasts or lunches. I continued moderating these events virtually during this period.

In early May, as news of potential border closures emerged (once again), I worried about the possibility of being trapped in the wrong place (once again). I discussed with my family the option of spending a few months back home in the countryside, where the shutdown felt less restrictive than in any big city. Since 2001, when I briefly returned to Munich before moving to San Francisco, I hadn't spent an extended period in Germany. Before traveling home – which, as a German citizen, was still feasible without health-related restrictions – I flew back to the tri-state area to retrieve a new set of clothes. Finding a reasonably priced flight of less than 20 hours' total duration from Mexico to Munich and without multiple transfers had become increasingly difficult, so I opted for a stopover in New York to update my wardrobe.

Arriving in New York, I was struck by a stark and unsettling transformation. The city, once vibrant and dynamic, had deteriorated into something far graver than before I'd left. This was a different-level escalation. The area around Port Authority Bus Terminal was eerily deserted, with only a scattering of homeless individuals and a few drug addicts mingling at the entrances. On one occasion, when wanting to catch a bus to Weehawken, New Jersey, where I was staying temporarily, I encountered a row of police officers stationed at the entrance. They were searching for a suspect, adding to the growing sense of unease. It all seemed like directly taken out of a ghastly thriller.

The terminal itself was ghostly quiet, with parts of it shut off completely. This was a far cry from the usual scene of Port Authority, where thousands of travelers hustled through daily. Previously, this terminal usually served about 8,000 buses and 225,000 passengers on an average weekday! While navigating through the crowds during a last-minute rush might have been a hassle then, the current emptiness was disheartening, a visible testament to the impact of mass manipulation and its consequences.

Midtown, normally a chaotic whirlwind of activity, had become a deserted ghost town. Times Square, usually brimming with masses of both locals and tourists that made it hard to move through, had now transformed into an empty expanse. The subway station, with its long, vacant tunnels and only the occasional figure in the distance, was almost unrecognizable. If you've ever experienced Times Square, you know the underground world: a maze of overcrowded tunnels, packed transfer corridors with street musicians, and congested platforms teeming with passengers, which often made it challenging to exit or board a train at rush hour. Seeing it so desolate was both surreal and sorrowful.

Broadway, once alive with its dazzling lights, now stood in somber darkness. The shop windows along the once-glamorous 5th Avenue were barricaded and boarded up. Union Square, usually a swarming hub of booths, farmers' markets, chess players, monks, and street performers, had become a ghostly stretch with only a few lonely travelers drifting through.

On a brighter note, Harlem's outdoor gatherings were making a comeback. Many restaurants had expanded their outdoor seating during the early months of lockdown, and the streets began to pulse with renewed energy and life.

Eventually, it was time for my flight to Germany. Upon arrival, I was asked to quarantine – a crazy thought, but it didn't disrupt my plans since I was headed straight to the village anyway. That summer was a beautiful return to my roots, spent in the village where I grew up, surrounded by the love of my family and the stunning landscapes of home. I borrowed a bike from my brother Franz and often went for rides, sometimes venturing on longer tours with my friend Gabi. We also organized reunions with "old friends" I hadn't seen in decades, reviving cherished memories.

Over the next 24 months, I stayed active with numerous online projects, maintaining connections across Africa and the U.S. I co-hosted a leadership-focused webinar series with Justine Chinoperekweyi from Zimbabwe (then working out of UAE), collaborating with UNICAF Zambia. I also took part in virtual events like one with Senamile Masango from South Africa and spoke at several events for major U.S. banks.

By the end of 2020, I decided to return to the U.S., this time to Miami Beach. I started with an Airbnb, then moved to another one for a few months before settling into an 8-month rental on Lenox Avenue. It wasn't long before I found where to dance Kizomba, Semba, and Kompa - mostly in the Hollywood area but also in South Beach, like at Sunday night events in South Pointe Park. Finally, I was dancing again! However, as time went on, the Kizomba scene started getting strange, with some organizers concerned about others who hadn't been injected. That wasn't what I was looking for, so I began to distance myself. That was the last thing I wanted!

Thankfully, I had my bike, which quickly became my best companion. I rode it almost every night after work, often stopping at the outdoors gym at Flamengo Park for a little extra exercise and then either taking the Venetian Way over to Miami or continuing north toward the golf course and into the residential areas all the way to W47th St. or La Gorce. I'd take longer rides on weekends over to Coconut Grove or Little Havana, or up the coast on the Beach Boardwalk. Sometimes I was caught in sudden tropical downpours, getting drenched to the bone. I remember one time, the flooding was knee-high within minutes as I tried to bike back from Brickell. I had to take refuge under the roof of a museum before braving the floods towards the Venetian Way to reach Miami Beach, where even the sidewalks were submerged. That day, I was so relieved to finally step into a hot shower and put on dry clothes. It wasn't the only time I found myself waiting out the rain under one of those enormous rubber trees along the way, which offered only temporary shelter from the storm.

Collins Park's palm trees framed the ideal backdrop for outdoor yoga classes held in front of the BASS Museum on Monday and Wednesday nights. Even better, these sessions were offered by the city free of charge.

I also made great friends with my upstairs neighbors, Justin and Meghan, and their golden retriever, Murphy. I absolutely adored this dog. He'd often stop at my door or peer through the window, and I'd take him for evening walks or look after him while they were away on a vacation trip. To this day, I still miss this guy, and he still pricks up his ears when he hears my name.

I frequently traveled back to New York to retrieve belongings from storage. There still was no significant networking there, so I was spending more time in Florida, while my business remained based in New York City. I figured I'd sort out any additional logistics later. For these flights, I mastered the art of "eating two celery sticks in two hours on airplanes" – if you know what I mean. After all, you cannot "passively eat," can you?

In 2021, with Miami's housing market booming and hyperinflation looming on the horizon, I decided to buy a newly renovated, fully furnished, and beautifully decorated condo in Miami Beach. It was leased to a tenant, whose rent covered mine with a little profit on top. Located in a prime area within a historic building near Lincoln Road, it seemed like a perfect investment. With so many New Yorkers and others flocking to Florida, the market was skyrocketing. Within a year, property values and rents would increase by 30%!

But things took a drastic turn. The condo owners in my building fell victim to a complex scheme that involved numerous people (I have some strong suspicions). One late Friday afternoon, the building was abruptly shut down by the City of Miami Beach. It took us 18 months to extricate ourselves, during which time we newer buyers suffered significant losses. After endless hours of stress, we finally managed to sell, though certainly not at market value and after paying 18 months of maintenance (what for?) without being able to rent or use our condos – occupied by squatters instead. Surely, the building's "unsafe structures" (?) were safe enough for *them*. At least, the City didn't seem to have a problem with them breaking in, while we owners were barred from accessing the property. Over time, the squatters stole what was sellable and ruined the rest, in league with the rats who also took advantage of the abandoned building. With the tenants having left in such a hurry, food had been left behind, and without electricity, the place became a paradise for pests.

When some of us tried to fight back, no lawyer would take our case without a hefty prepayment, and the press wouldn't touch it. The whole ordeal stank to high heaven. Every corner I poked into reeked of corruption. A friend in real estate once joked, "Miami – a sunny place for shady people." I wish I'd heard that, and from an expert like him, before I bought there. (He was referring to real estate deals.)

I won't burden you with more details, though I have plenty – dubious "official reports," hundreds of photos, videos, reluctance by the board to bring in experts outside those suggested by the management firm – I documented everything I could get my hands on. But that's beside the point, my point being…

What truly mattered was that my perseverance and faith saw me through. I've battled corruption before, but this time, despite my best efforts, I didn't succeed. It took time to recover from the shock of feeling helpless, but I emerged stronger and more resilient. Nothing can destroy me if I don't allow it. You can take away my possessions or money or residency permit, as happened before in Brazil, or my favorite activities, as happened in New York in 2020, but you can NEVER take away my power – unless I hand it to you, and I never will.

This experience cast a shadow over sunny Miami Beach for me. I never quite felt "at home" there, but I loved the tropical climate, lush vegetation, and the proximity to the ocean, where I could swim anytime, hurricanes permitting. The climate, vegetation, and nearby beaches were reminiscent of Rio de Janeiro, yet Miami Beach wasn't Rio.

The building drama began in January 2022, but the fall of 2021 was calm (yet eventful.) Inspired by a friend's experience and my own love for dogs – without the commitment of ownership due to frequent travels – I chose not to renew my lease and instead opted to pet-sit for a few months while figuring out my next destination. Eager to resume my travels and work from anywhere, I booked gigs in Denver, El Paso, and Merritt Island. In each location, I had a house to myself and, typically, access to a bike or car, my only housemates being the pets. In Denver, it was four large cats and two not-so-large dogs, with one of the cats always up for a "cat fight." El Paso brought me two tiny woolly companions, while Merritt Island introduced me to a large golden retriever, with whom I quickly bonded.

However, an accident involving the golden retriever in Merritt Island sent me to the emergency room with a fractured wrist. Not going into the details of that emergency room, but it was bad, with no specialized doctor available to treat my injury! At least, they didn't request any proof of you-know-what… After making it back to Miami, I spent a few weeks recovering at my friend Barbie's house in Hialeah, one of the kindest and most generous souls I know, who promptly picked me up from the airport and provided support during my recovery. As a side, isn't it amazing how the Universe placed her on my path just a few months earlier, literally days before I left for Colorado? Somehow, despite some of the "tough lessons" I've co-created for myself in this lifetime, I've also always been miraculously protected and supported…

Just two days after my surgery, the unimaginable happened: the building housing my condo was shut down by the City of Miami Beach, marking the beginning of the 18-month saga I've described earlier. Yet, there's a light at the end of the tunnel. We just must be willing to see it.

In the summer of 2022, wanting a break from it all and seeking respite and clarity, I felt like physical distance from it all could be helpful. So, I returned to Germany for a while to fully focus on my work and my dearest personal relationships. I feel blessed to say that my childhood home would always welcome me with open arms, offering a serene refuge, a true paradise during the warmer months with its view on the mountains, ample biking trails, beautiful lakes, rivers, and breathtaking hikes just a short drive away. The fresh, organic produce from the garden was a delightful bonus – the cherry on the cake!

But there was another pull: the call of Africa had grown too loud to ignore. I initially planned a three-month stay starting in Zanzibar. However, after a month there, I cut my visit short for personal reasons unrelated to my intended destinations and returned briefly to Germany before heading back to Miami Beach. More on that in the next chapter.

Leadership Wisdom – Key Takeaways

Never Give up Freedom for Safety, or You Will Lose Both

Sacrificing your freedom for a sense of safety always leads to losing both. True security comes from standing up for your freedom. This sometimes includes embracing risk and uncertainty. Confinement is never an option; it only provides a false sense of safety while eroding your freedom. In fact, there is no freedom in following orders without a solid reason. Whether or not there is such a reason, sometimes requires a little research and at other times, just simple common sense, or both. And there is no freedom in following orders – neither now nor in the future. True freedom comes from free will – it's no coincidence both words share 'free.' By thinking for yourself, questioning so-called "authorities," and using your intuition – a true form of freedom – rather than blindly following a narrative, and by rejecting unnecessary restrictions or impositions while confronting challenges directly, you safeguard your freedom and build genuine resilience. Embrace risks that align with your values, and you'll cultivate a stronger, more secure sense of self, paving the way for real growth and progress. While doing so, you are making a critical contribution to the freedom of all humans. As you know by now: Everything I do is in the service of freedom, so this takeaway should come as no surprise.

Freedom to me also means being unattached to any seemingly (and often falsely) safe routines or traditions. While I do not oppose traditions in general – many of them make perfect sense – I do maintain that it's worth questioning them before putting them into practice, rather than blindly continuing to do something "as it's always been done" just *because*. There's the story of the woman who invites her friends for dinner. She serves a turkey. At one of her guest's query about why she cut the ends off the turkey, the young woman realized she has no clear reason. Curious, she asks her mother the next day, only to learn that the practice was a tradition passed down from her grandmother. As it eventually turns out, grandma's pot was too small for the entire turkey. This revelation makes both women aware that the tradition no longer has any practical purpose as they both own plenty of large pots. It is simply a family custom that has never been questioned.

The same goes for many traditions and customs, especially those that cause harm to certain groups. It's time to question and change them. If you encounter such practices within your sphere of influence, I encourage you to engage actively in fostering transformation. While the process may be challenging, the potential to effect positive change for others is immensely rewarding – provided that it is done with respect for others' autonomy and without imposing unwelcome changes. Ultimately, it is a matter of upholding the principles of freedom, choice, and free will.

Finding Opportunity in "Adversity"

Any time "adversity" strikes, I ask myself, "How is this happening *for* me?" (rather than *to* me) and "What healing do I need to bring about for myself?" Now, I won't pretend I didn't initially react with frustration and anger when I noticed I was running up against a wall – I did! I was genuinely shaken and didn't feel *freakin' amazing* at all. I cursed and shouted and protested! But I soon remembered my own teachings, and the question emerged from my heart: "How is this happening *for* me?"

I'm not suggesting that we should remain passive when we're wronged or mistreated. Standing up for ourselves and setting clear boundaries is essential. However, clinging to feelings of hate or anger doesn't benefit us. It's important to assert our rights while also letting go of negativity to maintain our own well-being. We can move from *freakin' out* to *freakin' amazing* by embracing vulnerability, accepting support from friends, tapping into our own strength and resourcefulness, and affirming our intrinsic power. The situation may have been caused by someone else (our "teachers") but overwhelm (our reaction) is self-created. Meaning, we can also discreate it.

The reason the word "adversity" is within quotation marks above is that I want us to consider whether it is really *that*. What if it could lead us to something extraordinary? So, the next time you face a setback, shift your perspective. Consider how it might contribute to your growth and what lessons it holds. So-called adversity often hides an opportunity. Embrace the challenge, reach out for support as needed, and most importantly, ask yourself: "How is this happening *for* me?" and "What do I need to heal right now?"

No One Can Take Your Power Away

You might mentally disconnect from your power, but no one can take it from you, and no one can give it (back) to you because you have never given it away. You simply can't give your power away; it remains

176

within you, always accessible and available, though it may be temporarily dormant.

Similarly, no one can empower you but yourself. Beware of people who say they want to "empower you." They may either misunderstand the concept they're talking about, misuse the term, or even attempt to manipulate you. Rather than "empowering you," a coach or friend's role is to *guide* you in reconnecting with your intrinsic power, which essentially means "empowering yourself."

You are never powerless; you cannot lose or relinquish your power. You can only become disconnected from it. Just like a power cord needs to be plugged in for energy to flow, when you're disconnected from your power, you allow others' weaknesses to influence or even govern your life. Always remember to plug in your power cord so your power energy can flow freely.

You don't need to reclaim your power from outside of you because you never lost it. If you feel like you lost your power, that's because it has simply been dormant, in you, waiting for you to reconnect and "do its thing" (again). Harnessing your power this way is a sign of proactiveness, not reactiveness.

*

As I packed my bags for Zanzibar, my anticipation was palpable. Finally, I'd be stepping onto African soil again! I'd arranged a month-long stay in an Airbnb in Zanzibar Town, blending work with island life. I devoured YouTube videos, eager to dive into its unique blend of cultures and experiences. I wanted to not just get a faint taste of this spice island but immerse myself in its flavors and essence.

Chapter 25

Savoring Zanzibar: A Symphony of Spice and Flavor

Lessons in the Heart's Voice, Curiosity, Valuing Local Wisdom, and Gratitude

At Abeid Amani Karume International Airport, the Airbnb driver awaited my arrival. The Airbnb in Zanzibar City, owned by a warm and welcoming local family who lived on the ground floor, was managed by Petra, who had kindly arranged for the driver to pick me up. Our first stop was a local bank to exchange currency. The line was long, but the driver waited patiently with me before we continued on to the house. For the month in Freddie Mercury's birth town, I had my own room and bathroom but shared the kitchen and living space with two other guests and Petra. A unique feature of my stay was the free wake-up call: the muezzin's call to prayer echoing from the loudspeakers of a nearby mosque, punctually at dawn (around 5:20am) and again at sunrise (6:30am).

After settling in, unpacking my essentials, and refreshing in the shower, I prepared to check out the labyrinthic structure of Stone Town, which was just a 10-minute walk away. Starving, I stopped at a small restaurant and enjoyed a spicy curry on their cozy outdoor deck. I only got a brief taste of Stone Town that day because I was a bit tired from the trip. Also, Petra had arranged a *tuk-tuk* (also called *bajajis*) to take me to a distant grocery store that evening, where I could pick up some additional essentials like olive oil, coffee, and cheese, which I hadn't found nearby. While I'm usually adaptable, I love salads, especially in warm weather, and I prefer them with olive oil. Plus, the *tuk-tuk* ride promised to be a nice little sightseeing tour as well. It didn't disappoint – not because of the store itself, but because of what we saw along the way. It was Mwaka Kogwa, the festival celebrating the New Year according to the Shirazi calendar, and the streets were alive with people in festive attire, especially the women and girls. It felt like a colorful fashion show unfolding before my eyes. The driver, whose name I regrettably forgot, was an incredibly agile *tuk-tuk* driver and a very kind man. I was taken aback when I later saw him open the small door to his seat and realized he had no legs.

The next day, I headed to Darajani Market to stock up on fresh fruits and vegetables. I was thrilled to find piles of yellow passion fruit, just like those I knew from Rio de Janeiro – I bought two pounds on the spot! I quickly learned that prices varied significantly, and it didn't take long to figure out who was trying to charge me tourist rates and who wasn't. By the end of my first visit, I had already identified my favorite sellers, though I hadn't made it through the entire market that afternoon. Zanzibar is a paradise for spices, and Darajani offers a vast selection. I picked up the basics and made a mental note to return before heading home to buy more for my mom and siblings.

Just outside the largest hall, there were stalls selling delicious dates, which soon became my go-to snack for the month, along with a large bag of cashew nuts. Darajani Bazaar is an expansive market, with the main hall and surrounding outdoor areas occupying an entire block, and the bazaar itself spilling into multiple streets and alleys. The market alone is worth a visit to Zanzibar Town – it's always an experience! Some of the sellers would often toss a few extra tomatoes or herbs into my bag. One day, an old man selling fresh peas added an extra handful to my purchase, despite having shelled them one by one. On another visit, a man with a large wooden cart invited me to hop on so he could give me a ride around the market. I declined, but we shared a hearty laugh.

I discovered a yoga mat tucked away on the living room shelves and decided to practice on the rooftop occasionally to avoid getting rusty while traveling. One morning, on my mat, I was astonished to see a man painting the façade of a nearby building. He maneuvered precariously on makeshift scaffolding with no safety measures – no railings, nets, or ropes – on the fourth floor. At one point, he even jumped from a balcony onto the wooden boards around the corner. I found myself holding my breath, not from a yoga technique, but from sheer awe and anxiety, hoping he wouldn't fall. It was a stark reminder of how many people risk their lives daily to earn a few dollars to sustain their families.

On my daily walks, I quickly befriended a friendly tailor whose modest shop opened onto the small dirt road leading to our house. With my limited Swahili vocabulary – words like "habari" (hello, how are you?), "nzuri" (good), "mambo" (how's it going?), "asante sana" (thank you very much), "karibu" (welcome), and a few essential numbers – I managed to connect with the locals, sometimes regretting I hadn't studied more. The numbers were especially handy when buying water from the guys at a beverage outlet down the street or picking up my favorite sesame-covered bread, carefully wrapped in newspaper by the handsome young vendor at a tiny bread and burger stand on the road to Stone Town. One time, as I unwrapped the bread at home, I noticed that the magazine it was wrapped in had a cover that read "Love Bites." – How fitting!

My walks through the labyrinth of Stone Town quickly became a cherished routine. I'd wander the winding alleys, memorizing landmarks to help me find my way back, and after a few days, my sense of direction was spot on. During one of these strolls, I met Ema, a local artist who later gifted me a beautiful painting he'd created specifically for me – again, lovingly wrapped in newspaper.

Evenings often found me at the Forodhani Night Food Market, a lively place where tables overflowed with fresh fish, seafood, and local delicacies. The Zanzibar pizza was a crowd favorite, but my personal obsession became the Urojo Soup (Zanzibar Mix). For about a dollar, it was the perfect meal and my absolute favorite in Zanzibar. I even joke these days that if anyone knew how to cook it, I'd marry him on the spot! Speaking of which, the area around the food market and Darajani Park was always teeming with young, very handsome guys, hoping to catch the eye of a female visitor – though likely for the wrong reasons, given the age difference. A couple of them insisted again and again that I should join them for a dance night out. I declined, and they didn't take it very well, but we're not supposed to please everyone, are we?

A spectacle not to be missed was the group of young Zanzibari kids performing acrobatic dives into the harbor, not far from the food market. I could have watched them for hours! Another local treasure were the chapatis made by women on the narrow sidewalks of Old Town – fresh, juicy, and by far the best (and cheapest) around… always wrapped in newspaper for the extra flavor!

One day, I decided to take the *dala-dala* (a van crammed full of passengers) to Nungwi Beach for a day. It was an awesome journey through many picturesque villages and landscapes. One of my favorite things to do while traveling is to take in everyday life along the way – how people live, the way they travel, their villages and houses, and all the little details that reveal the rhythm of a place.

When walking from the *dala-dala* to the beach, I encountered one of the many motorbike taxi riders on a corner listening to some Ndombolo music. I couldn't help but walk up to him and show off a few dance moves. We shared a dance, a laugh and a little chat before I continued on my way. Shortly after, I saw a place with some simple, nice cottages for rent, and I decided to book one for a night the following week, as I wanted to go swimming with the dolphins, which turned out to be a – ma – zing!

For that next visit to the beach town, the owner of my Airbnb had business to take care of in Nungwi, so he gave me a ride. I toured the area for the rest of the day, visited the Maasai village, and booked the boat trip for the following day. While it was a relatively chilly day out on the boat, swimming with the dolphins in the open sea was a whole other level of experience! Just spectacular! We jumped in the water with two different pods along the way. On our boat trip back, we saw uncountable starfish, and we also stopped for great snorkeling at a sand bank.

Another day, I hired a driver I'd met in Stone Town to take me to Jozani Forest, where I went on a fascinating tour with a guide who explained the myriad plants, each with its own medicinal purpose. This forest literally provides a plant for any ailment you could possibly think of. The forest is also home to the unique Red Colobus monkey, with its long tail and curious demeanor. We were lucky to see several of them.

When I asked the driver for a good place to dance in Zanzibar Town, he recommended Tatu (which means "three"), a three-story venue with a restaurant on the ground floor, a bar and billiards on the second, and a nightclub on the third. One night, despite being tired from a boat trip to Prison Island (with its giant turtles), I decided to check it out. As I climbed the stairs to the second floor, I couldn't believe my eyes – there, playing billiards, was my artist friend from Johannesburg, Reggie Khumalo! What are the odds? It was perfect synchronicity, as it happened to be his last day on the island.

Though Reggie had to leave early due to work commitments, we played a round of billiards to kick off the night. I hadn't played in ages – well, except for that one time in Morocco when I somehow won most of my games against a local. My first shots were surprisingly good this time, too, but soon enough, my luck ran out… though not my good mood. And so it was that I met Evodia, who invited me to hang out at Paje beach, where she usually stayed.

Another afternoon, I was sitting on one of the concrete benches at the Old Fort's amphitheater when two students suddenly flanked me, later joined by a third. Initially, I thought they were the usual "I want to walk with you" types, but no – they wanted to interview me for their studies. They were training to become professional tourist guides, and our conversation turned into an inspirational session. They were incredibly receptive and open-minded (as I've often found African youth to be) and thanked me for being their "teacher" (or coach?).

During another visit to the Old Fort, I watched a group of dancers rehearsing their routines. One of them, Brown, struck up a conversation with me about dance and their performances. We decided to exchange moves – he'd teach me a few Afrobeat moves, and I'd show him some Ndombolo. Brown was super athletic and a phenomenal dancer and acrobat, yet humble. He told me that dancing was how he supported himself and his sisters back on the Tanzanian mainland.

We met up at the amphitheater a few times to dance, and it was a blast. We also had long chats before I left. Unfortunately, after returning from Zanzibar, I lost track of him – he must have changed his phone number. If you ever travel to Zanzibar and meet dancer Brown (he performs at many hotels on the beach), please do say hi.

I frequently struck up conversations with random people on the streets – or they with me, like two waitresses I met during my stay. One I encountered at a traffic light, and we ended up walking together for a while; the other was working at a small outdoor bar at the Old Fort. Both seemed to be seeking advice – I must have had "coach" written on my forehead…

Although my plans were initially to take the ferry to Dar es-Salaam on the Tanzanian mainland for a meeting with a business connection and then continue my journey to other countries, personal reasons led me to cut my trip short and return to Germany sooner than expected. But before leaving, I decided to take a day trip to Paje on the eastern coast. My *tuk-tuk* driver friend took me to Mwanakwerekwe Market, where he made sure I got on the right *dala-dala* to head east. The ride was an experience in itself – the most rundown *dala-dala* I'd ever been on. I sat in the back row, my feet resting on bags filled with who knows what, surrounded by seats that looked as though they'd been in use for a thousand years. A tall Maasai man slept open-mouthed in the row ahead of me, adding to the flavor.

When I finally arrived in Paje, I sought out the restaurant where the lady from Tatu, Evodia, worked. We enjoyed breakfast at a small spot and then took a long, leisurely walk on the beach. Later, back at the hotel's outdoor bar, the DJ was napping on one of the benches. He soon joined us, along with the female cook, and we turned the rest of the afternoon into an impromptu happy hour. Eventually, it was time to say my goodbyes and catch the *dala-dala* back home – a process that took much longer than expected. After a long wait, I finally boarded one, only to discover near the end of the journey that I needed to transfer to another. Fortunately, the driver kindly helped me make the connection, and I reached my destination just in time for a casual online meeting I had scheduled for that night.

Hungry and exhausted, I was relieved to find the boys on the corner still grilling the last two corncobs. I bought one – slightly dry but good enough – and headed back to my room to have the meeting and then pack up for my flight the next morning.

Leadership Wisdom – Key Takeaways

Never Dismiss Your Heart's Voice or You Might Miss Your Best Opportunities

The encounter with Reggie at Tatu offers a valuable lesson: Trusting your intuition can lead to unexpected and enriching experiences. When your inner voice nudges you to step out, like to a networking event, even when you're tempted to stay in, it's often guiding you toward something meaningful. Embrace these moments and let curiosity lead the way. You might discover opportunities and connections you never anticipated. Tune in to your instincts – they often know where the real adventure lies... or your best business opportunities!

Harness the Power of Curiosity for a Deeper Experience

From the varied experiences in Zanzibar – from dancing with Brown to sharing some Ndombolo moves with the motorbike taxi driver – there's a clear lesson in adaptability. Being curious and open to spontaneous opportunities and flexible in your plans can uncover unexpected benefits and connections. In both personal and professional settings, allowing room for serendipity can lead to valuable experiences and opportunities that a rigid approach might miss. Embrace the unplanned and be ready to pivot; it can often lead to the most rewarding experiences and outcomes.

Value Local Insights and Connections

In Zanzibar, interacting with locals at markets, food stalls, and cultural sites demonstrated the importance of leveraging local knowledge. The connections made with individuals like the vendor at

Darajani Market or the insightful students at the Old Fort show how valuable local perspectives can be. In leadership and business, seeking and valuing local insights can provide a deeper understanding of the environment and uncover opportunities that are not immediately obvious. Building relationships with those who know the landscape can enhance decision-making and lead to more informed and effective strategies.

Be Grateful and Appreciate What You Have to Get More of It

In Zanzibar, as I practiced yoga on the rooftop, I witnessed a man painting the façade of a nearby building. His safety gear was non-existent; he maneuvered precariously on rudimentary scaffolding with no railings or ropes, and even leaped from a balcony. Watching him, I was struck by the stark contrast between his risk-laden job and the relative comfort of my own situation.

This encounter served as a poignant reminder of the importance of appreciating what we have. The painter risked his life daily to support his family, while I enjoyed a secure environment and the luxury of choice in how I spent my days (even if not all of it had come easy). His courage and resilience highlighted how often we take our own comforts for granted.

In business and leadership, recognizing and valuing the resources and opportunities available to you can lead to greater success and fulfillment. When you show genuine appreciation for what you have – whether it's your team, your tools, or your skills – you cultivate a mindset that attracts more of the same. This appreciation not only enhances your current situation but also opens doors to new possibilities and improvements.

So, take a moment to reflect on your own circumstances. What aspects of your work, your team, or your environment do you sometimes overlook? By valuing these elements, you create a positive cycle that invites growth and abundance. Appreciate what you have and watch how it grows and enriches your life including your business or career.

*

As I flew home, I felt a pang of regret for missing out on mainland Tanzania. At the same time, I looked forward to a few more days of hiking and biking in Bavaria, my old stomping grounds. I was eager to savor some precious moments with my family before heading back to Miami Beach, where I would need to find a new place to stay until the building situation was sorted out and I'd be completely liberated to start a new chapter.

Chapter 26
The Butterfly Is Growing New Wings

Lessons in True Transformation

After spending some quality time with family and handling important matters in Germany, it was time to crawl out of the cocoon and head back to Miami Beach. Upon arrival, I spent a night at an aparthotel on Española Way before settling into my new home on Euclid Avenue, where I'd stay until August 2023.

The months leading up to the sale of the condo were nerve-wracking, an arduous process involving all 26 owners who had to agree, sign documents, and navigate the relentless tactics of the buyers. I'd hired a lawyer who did his part, though he could have been more effective toward the end. As I mentioned earlier, I'll spare you the details – they're just too absurd to believe.

On a brighter note, the Haitian Kompas Festival at Bayfront Park in Downtown Miami was on the horizon in May, celebrating its 25th anniversary. This festival is a big deal for Kompa lovers, drawing more than 25 bands and artists to the stage that day, including some of my favorites: Klass, TVice, and Nu Look. I ventured out early when some of the lesser-known artists were still playing, but the audience grew later as the stars were expected. Li te gwo… I had a *freakin' amazing* time among the Haitian crowd, wishing Chris could have been there to enjoy it with me and dance a little.

I met a nice Haitian man from another state who told me about an additional big event happening the next day: Madame Gougouse Haiti Cup Final at the North Miami Stadium. I bought a ticket, took the bus up, and when I arrived, I realized I was the only non-Haitian there. Fun fact: The security guard at the entrance was so surprised to see a non-Haitian woman like me show up alone that he forgot to scan my ticket. The whole place smelled of delicious Haitian food, two teams were playing soccer, and the stage was set at the far end of the venue. I had a look around the entire area and soon ran into my new friend before the concert began. To my excitement, Klass was performing again! That weekend was definitely a musical highlight.

When the sale was finally sealed, I felt a wave of relief wash over me - despite the loss, the betrayal, and the countless hours spent on this saga. I reminded myself that everything happens *for* me, not *to* me. This shift in perspective allowed me to start reflecting on the lessons learned, both mentally and emotionally. I no longer felt the need to stay close to the building, constantly monitoring the situation, and was finally ready to leave Miami Beach behind.

But before cleaning out the apartment, with renewed energy and a clear mind, I found myself reconnecting with people more proactively. I couldn't have asked for a better day than the one I spent with Scott Ferguson, a brilliant new friend who also happens to be a top-rated podcast host (I'd guested on his show), coach, and real estate investor. Scott didn't hesitate to drive all the way down the coast from Palm Beach Gardens to meet me in South Beach, and we made the most of our time together. We spent the entire day deep in conversation, masterminding as we strolled through the quiet streets of South Beach, sipped kava at a local bar, indulged in a delicious Italian lunch on 5th Street and dessert on Ocean Drive, and shared our plans for the near future. There's something truly special about meeting someone in person after only knowing them online – it's like the connection suddenly becomes real, tangible, and infinitely more meaningful.

With the "building" chapter closed, I was free to reinvest. The question was: where? New York City no longer seemed like a viable option, given its current challenges. The city, in my eyes, had lost a lot of its value, despite property prices remaining sky-high. Miami, too, was on the verge of a potential real estate bubble, and the vibrant dance scenes I once loved had dwindled in both places. France began to surface in my thoughts, particularly Paris – a city I'd always envisioned as a potential home. But there were also reasons to hesitate, rooted in research I won't go into here. So, I asked myself: what's the next-biggest, equally beautiful city in France that offers a strong African dance scene? The answer was clear – Lyon (though I'd never been there). And just like that, I booked a flight for the summer of 2023 to explore Lyon, see if it could be a fit for my investment, and if so, find a place to buy.

Before my departure, a special highlight brightened my final days in Miami Beach. Chris, my favorite Kompa dancer and close friend, announced he was coming to visit. We hadn't seen each other since March 2020, the day after my birthday, so the news had me over the moon! He planned to stay with me for the weekend, and we were excited to dance the night away at a Kompa event up in Hollywood. I'll never forget the moment Chris pulled up in his rental car. We shared a heartfelt hug that felt like no time had passed. And here's the *freakin' amazing* part – today, as I write this very chapter, it happens to be Chris's birthday! Talk about synchronicity! It's moments like these that remind me how mysteriously the Universe works, constantly filling life with unexpected connections and "coincidences." I swear I had not planned for this magical timing. It's just divine! Sak pase, zanmi mwen? (I love the sound of Haitian Creole!)

We spent a wonderful weekend together, indulging in fresh quiche from the local French bakery, strolling along South Beach, dancing to live Kompa music until the early hours (and hunting for a parking spot when back home), and talking about my dream of visiting his homeland, Haiti, someday. We capped it off with a laid-back happy hour and late lunch at Nikki Beach on Sunday afternoon. It was the perfect way to add a *freakin' amazing* final note to my time in Miami Beach.

With only a few days left, I packed up the last of my belongings and moved them to Hialeah with the help of my dear friend Barbie. She finally dropped me off at Miami International Airport for my flight to Lyon, where I was surprised to find the city so empty. As it turns out, many Lyonnais leave the city in the summer for the surrounding mountains or the beach. Unfortunately, there wasn't much dancing to be found, though I did manage to catch a Kizomba event one night! The African dance classes, however, wouldn't start until October – oh là là là là! A bit disappointing, but I still fell in love with the city and the prospect of learning Sabar, the Senegalese dance, in the absence of Congolese Ndombolo. And if I ever felt the need, I knew Paris was just a quick two-hour TGV ride away, where I could always take classes with Tshamala Mbongo, as I'd done on a previous visit.

When my time at the first Airbnb near Perrache train station was up, I moved to a charming place on Les Pentes, the hillside area that leads up to Croix Rousse. I was still on the hunt for the right investment property. Initially, I was drawn to a beautiful apartment near Place Sathonay, despite it lacking a complete kitchen. The large living room, with its open fireplace and beautiful stucco ceiling, enchanted me, and the location was perfect. Beauty always gets me! However, after doing some research, I discovered that the property had been on the market for an unusually long time, which set off alarms. My intuition told me something was off with the building, so I decided to steer clear. Instead, I opted for a smaller place with a garden – a tradeoff, but the outdoors area also was a luxury I hadn't had since leaving my parents' house. It was in a different neighborhood that, while not my first choice, turned out to be conveniently close to my favorite dance activities. Although in Lyon, nothing is really that far. Once that was settled, and while waiting for the closing date, I decided to travel again.

I returned to Lyon toward the end of October for the closing and to start my Sabar dance classes with Pape and Lilou at AfroMundo. In November, I traveled to Paris for a Congolese show. During that trip, I took classes with Tshamala and his live musicians, and at breakfast in my hotel, I met Loick, a young Congolese man who quickly became one of my first friends in France – a heaven-sent person, kind, generous, and open-minded. December brought me back to Miami, and then, over the next few months, it was Lyon, Marseille, New York, and Munich in quick succession. Dance-wise, I also took advantage of some excellent Guinean and West African workshops, and a little Afro House. I recently even found a new companion for Ndombolo here, Lynda, a young Congolese woman, who I sometimes practice with.

Now, as I sit at my desk in Lyon, finishing this book and gazing out at my garden, I occasionally spot a lizard or a cat strolling by, reminding me of Miami Beach as there are plenty of both there, and I'm already dreaming of my next destinations.

I'm a *papillon* – a butterfly – now splitting my time, flying between France (Lyon) and the U.S. (Miami and New York City), but not without occasional visits to Germany and the African continent, while also trying to find the best moment to visit Brazil *para matar as saudades* (to relieve the nostalgia) and dance a few *Sambinhas*.

Leadership Wisdom – Key Takeaways

Every Situation Holds Two Lessons: Practical and Transformational

In every situation, there's both a practical lesson and a deeper, transformational one. From the Miami Beach ordeal, the practical lesson was clear: Don't jump at investing in a historic building in a prime Miami Beach location without digging into every detail – history, general setting, who's involved in its management, who's on the Board, what are the tenants' stories about it, who sits in the City's building department, who are the big players in the area, and all. You'll likely uncover irregularities and hidden agendas, and unless you have a stash of cash just lying around, you'd better do thorough research rather than relying on a real estate agent who's just in it to make a sale.

The transformational lesson is where things get more personal… and profound! It revolves around asking yourself, "How is this happening *for* me?" or "How has this happened *for* me?" or, if you prefer: "What's the purpose of this experience?" The answer is deeply personal and varies for everyone. If it's a recurring issue, it's often a pattern. For me, it's been about dealing with betrayal. Why does this keep happening? As I mentioned at the start of this book, my life isn't perfect; it's a work in progress – with "progress" being the key word. Focusing on progress means cultivating a growth mindset, but it goes deeper. Unless we achieve the same with a different method, we need to dig into our subconscious to unearth and eradicate the root beliefs that keep us stuck in repetitive patterns; the paradigms that have us experience the same, just in different shapes.

I've spent years uncovering these deep-seated beliefs, and I've helped many of my clients do the same, very successfully. And yet, there was still that one thing, that one hidden reason that was bringing back experiences of (perceived) loss and betrayal. I'm saying "perceived" because when you ask, "How is this happening *for* me?" you start to understand that there is no betrayal or loss.

- There is no real loss – only growth and winning.
- There is no betrayal – only teaching.
- There are no traitors – only teachers.
- There are no enemies – only allies in disguise.
- There are no annoying behaviors – only reflections in a mirror.

What felt like betrayal or loss magically turns into an opportunity to grow, to heal, and to rid yourself of "that one thing," once and for all!

I made a promise to myself that I'd uncover this root belief by the time I finished writing this book, and I did. And this is what living a *freakin' amazing life* is about.

This breakthrough is not only invaluable to me and my life going forward, but it will also significantly enrich the work I do with my clients. The deep insights I've gained will elevate the support and guidance I can offer them.

Chapter 27
From Transformation to Liberation

The Ultimate Lesson

Everything I do is in the service of one ultimate goal: freedom. And that freedom includes feeling *freakin' amazing* in your leadership role – leading yourself, and possibly also others around you.

Transformation is great. But a truly *freakin amazing life* doesn't stop there. It includes freedom. This isn't just about external freedom and not being physically imprisoned or restricted by rules we don't agree with. It's the inner freedom we (also) want to strive for. Because with it comes harmony, as we are now able to find peace in chaos.

Freedom also comes with responsibility – the ability to respond in ways that serve the greater good.

Freedom means recognizing that victimhood holds us back because everything in the past, present, and future unfolds for our growth; it happens *for* us.

While many people search for balance, I believe what they truly seek is harmony. Harmony is more achievable when we become neutral observers and alchemists, using feelings as indicators and emotions as catalysts. I don't claim to have mastered this art, but I'm a dedicated student, committed to making progress on this path. Because my ultimate goal is not just transformation, but liberation.

Today, as a Transformational Leadership Coach and CEO of TRANSFORM YOUR PERFORMANCE, I guide my clients to become *thriving* leaders – whether in corporate settings, non-profits, or as business owners leading their own teams. My approach helps them break through both internal and external barriers, elevate their leadership skills, and enhance their presence, enabling them to expand their influence, impact, income, and fulfillment while managing priorities and stress with greater ease. The result? A more rewarding leadership experience and happier, more engaged teams.

Self-leadership always comes first. It is the cornerstone of successful leadership. Without mastering it, we can't authentically model leadership, nor can we achieve sustainable success. Leading with authenticity and from the heart not only earns the respect of others but also allows us to reap greater fulfillment and satisfaction. It makes the leadership journey *freakin' amazing* – even when challenges arise. When my clients go all in and commit fully, they don't just transform their careers or businesses; they transform their entire lives. Leadership isn't just a role; it's a holistic experience, just as our entire life is a holistic phenomenon, where every part is interconnected. That's why my coaching approach is multidisciplinary and holistic.

My clients don't just report promotions and significant salary increases – $20,000, $30,000, $50,000, or more. Business owners see higher team loyalty and creativity, and they receive genuine praise for their leadership. But beyond professional gains, they also experience improvements in their personal lives: stronger relationships, less stress, better health, and even weight loss – areas we didn't directly focus on. They feel less worried and more joyful. Are joy and fulfillment something you'd like to feel more of as well?

In addition to one-on-one coaching, I also teach courses and workshops rooted in my coaching and leadership frameworks, sharing these powerful tools with a broader audience:

- Powerful Leadership Transformation (PLT)™
- New-Paradigm Leadership (NPL)™
- The T.H.R.I.V.I.N.G. Leader Formula (TTLF)™
- The Unique Assets Framework™
- The Negotiate Your Dream Salary Framework™.

What I personally love about my clientele is its rich diversity, which makes this work even more exciting for someone like me who thrives in change. I've had the pleasure of working with women and men from the United States, Africa, Asia, Europe, and Latin America, coaching and training in English, Spanish, Portuguese, and German. My multinational and multicultural background allows me to seamlessly connect with clients from a variety of cultural contexts.

My book *Speak up, Stand out and Shine: Speak Powerfully in Any Situation* has assisted thousands to excel in speaking engagements, from presentations and keynotes to panels, media appearances, negotiations, networking events, and job interviews. It's a valuable resource for anyone looking to overcome pre-speaking jitters or elevate their speaker presence. I invite you to check it out on Amazon.

As an International Inspirational Speaker, I've been told I inspire greatness, with some even claiming a single talk has changed their lives. Perhaps it's my knack for fresh perspectives and boldness, or maybe it's because I pour my heart and soul into every gig.

Additionally, I launched the *RISE TO LEAD* podcast to serve as a hub for leadership inspiration. Tune in for candid conversations and invaluable insights from bold leaders across industries and nations. I invite you to listen and absorb your dose of courageous leadership excellence and draw from these lessons to create conscious change and help shape the world with your audacious leadership footprint, leading with a bold heart – all in the service of greater freedom for yourself and those you get to impact.

If you're ready to level up your effectiveness and impact as a *thriving* leader, and to experience more joy, peace, satisfaction, success, and freedom in your daily leadership, let's connect! Scan the QR code to book a spot on my calendar or email me at regina@transformyourperformance.com if you don't find a convenient time slot.

If you're not quite ready to dive headfirst into the limitless potential of your brilliance and step fully into your greatness, that's okay – let's take the next step together. Click the link to download my *Create Your Freakin' Amazing Life Template*.

Regardless of where you are on your journey, I'd be honored to support you and can't wait to hear about the *Freakin' Amazing Life* you're about to create.

Epilogue

As I wrote this book, I found myself re-living many of the experiences that shaped me. Tears often streamed down my face – some from sadness, others from joy. The tears of sadness brought healing, while the tears of joy reminded me to smile. Thank you for allowing me to share these stories and lessons with you. I hope you found value in these glimpses into my *freakin' amazing life* and that the lessons I've learned serve you as well.

I wish I could sing "Je ne regrette rien" like Edith Piaf. There are, however, a few things I regret – mostly those I didn't do. Despite the vulnerability I've poured into writing this book, these regrets are deeply personal and not meant for public consumption. I mention them now in the hope that they might inspire you to avoid leaving anything undone that you might later regret.

Fortunately, my adventurous spirit, insatiable curiosity, and passion for exploring the world's mysteries have taken me to many places. I've traveled extensively, including to destinations not yet mentioned, such as Thailand and numerous countries in Europe and Latin America. Although living abroad has shortened the list of countries I'd otherwise have visited – since I often used my vacations to see family back home – it has provided me with a much deeper understanding of many places and cultures than a short stay could ever do.

Your dreams may be vastly different from mine. Perhaps travel isn't your passion; maybe you're drawn to creating something entirely different for yourself. What truly matters is that you pursue what you feel called to do, following your own passions and dreams; that you allow yourself to experience life fully – to create a life worth living and an existence worth being.

Yes, I have lived. You, too, can live your dreams!

You can create the life that's perfect for YOU – anywhere in the world!

THE END of this book – but not the end of my *Freakin' Amazing Life*!

Rather, a NEW BEGINNING.

Bring on the next chapter!

Poem – Part 2

Remember the poem from one of the first pages of the book? – Here's its continuation:

Someday, darling, we'll be gray

Darling, we'll be gray

And fret about the dreams we didn't chase

The roads not taken, the words unsaid,

The doors we closed, the paths we fled.

We'll wonder where those chances would've led,

And what we may have lost in fear and dread.

But in that twilight, as we gaze,

We'll know our story's still ablaze,

For every missed and silent chance,

Made room for life's unplanned dance.

And though the years have slipped away,

We find our spark in this new day,

It's never late to change the pace,

To chase the dreams we dared not face.

So now we turn, embrace our fate,

For even now, it's not too late.

The paths we feared, we now create,

And with each step, our *freakin' amazing* future waits.

Acknowledgments

My deepest gratitude goes to my loving and beloved parents, my two brothers Franz and Anton, my two sisters Rosmarie and Martina, and my nephews Felix, Tobias, and Moritz. I feel profoundly blessed to be part of such a caring and kindhearted family, and I am endlessly grateful for your unwavering support and cherished company along the way. My heart is filled with sweet memories, and every time I return to our farm, it truly feels like home and like a place of unconditional love. The warmth of my original home always reminds me of how fortunate I am.

A heartfelt thank you to Chris, my favorite friend and Kompa dance partner in New York. As you always said, we share a "special connection," and I can't imagine what I would have done without your presence, embrace, and support.

I also want to acknowledge other dear and loyal friends who have stood by me through some of the most challenging times: Ana María, Sabrina, Ahmyna, Raquel, Susan, Vicky, Liz, Lisa, Erika, Stéphanie, Justin and Meghan, and Barbie. Not to forget Ibrahima, who – like a messenger of happiness – appeared in my life in NYC and later welcomed me with open arms in Paris for a week of beautiful experiences. Your friendship and generosity have been a source of strength, and I am truly grateful for all of you.

About the Author

As the CEO of **TRANSFORM YOUR PERFORMANCE**, Regina Huber drives bold, heart-centered leadership. She helps her clients become thriving leaders by leveling up their leadership of self & others.

Her eclectic experience on five continents started in Germany and includes leadership positions at Boston Consulting Group (Europe, South America, U.S.) as well as ownership of businesses in Argentina, Brazil, and the U.S.

This experience shaped her into a multinational **Transformational Leadership Coach, International Inspirational Speaker**, and **Author** of *Speak up, Stand out and Shine* and *Living My Freakin' Amazing Life*. She also co-authored three other books and translated 13. She speaks five languages, along with some Italian, and studied Latin. She is the **Host** of the ***RISE TO LEAD*** **Podcast**.

Regina writes visionary articles for magazines internationally and is passionate about sharing wisdom and inspiration, earning features in multiple media outlets in the U.S., Latin America, Asia, and Africa. She was also the host of the *What's Your Spark* TV show.

Over the years, she has inspired audiences at events and taught workshops all over the world. She was an active Member of the Leadership Team of the Financial Women's Association (FWA) and has collaborated with numerous organizations internationally.

Regina created five proprietary coaching frameworks, inc. Powerful Leadership Transformation (PLT)™, New-Paradigm Leadership (NPL)™, and The T.h.r.i.v.i.n.g. Leader Formula (TTLF)™. She is certified in Conversational Intelligence (C-IQ)®, BodyTalk, Human Design, and other holistic methodologies.

She has a passion for travel, adventure, and dance.

Website: https://transformyourperformance.com

RISE TO LEAD Podcast:
https://transformyourperformance.com/podcast

- **On Apple:** https://podcasts.apple.com/us/podcast/rise-to-lead/id1755539127
- **On Spotify:** https://open.spotify.com/show/2p4AZukhopnUmwSI4WnSSE

LinkedIn: https://www.linkedin.com/in/reginahuber

YouTube: https://www.youtube.com/@reginahuber

Facebook: https://www.facebook.com/ReginaHuber369

Instagram: https://www.instagram.com/reginahubernyclyon

www.ingramcontent.com/pod-product-compliance
Lightning Source LLC
Chambersburg PA
CBHW070805050426
42452CB00011B/1907